Horst Hegewald-Kawich and Ginny Altman

The German Shepherd Dog

Everything About Purchase, Care, Feeding, and Training

Filled with Full-color Photographs
Illustrations by Michele Earle-Bridges

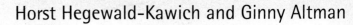

BARRON'S

CONTENTS

3

GENERAL DESCRIPTION OF THE GERMAN SHEPHERD DOG

The intelligence, strength, versatility, and beauty of the German Shepherd Dog are known all over the world. These characteristics have made the German Shepherd Dog one of the most popular dog breeds, not only in the United States of America, but also in the world.

Origin

As a purebred dog, the German Shepherd Dog is a relatively new breed developed in the late 1800s and early 1900s in Germany from the various stock and farm dogs in Germany and Europe. The breed ancestors were principally medium-sized, smooth-coated sheep dogs that demonstrated good character and a suitable work ethic, tirelessly moving sheep to pasture and guarding them from predators.

The beauty of the German Shepherd Dog has made it one of the world's most popular breeds.

Attributes

The German Shepherd Dog's most important attributes are its character and temperament. The German Shepherd Dog is a poised, confident, and faithful companion to man. The intelligence and aptitude for training of this breed are well known. This amazing versatility makes this breed suitable for many specialized services such as work as a service dog for the blind or physically handicapped, as a police dog, a narcotics detection dog, a war sentry dog, a therapy dog, or as a search and rescue dog. The dog's natural protective instincts make the dog a guardian of home, property, or livestock. The dog is indifferent to strangers and does not

The service dog works as an assistant to the physically handicapped.

give affection lightly but when its devotion is given, it is given for life. The German Shepherd Dog delights in serving as a companion, as a friend to children, as a partner of police and narcotics officers, and as canine team partners of our men and women in the armed services.

Size

The German Shepherd Dog is of medium size ranging from 22 inches to 24 inches (25–30 cm) for females and 24 inches to 26 inches (30–35 cm) for males. Both males and females that are larger than the ideal are seen regularly today but responsible breeders are not encouraging the increasing size of the dog.

Colors

There are a number of colors recognized.
✔ The most common is the black and tan or black and red. This is a color pattern in which the dog exhibits a black saddle and the feet and legs are tan or red. Black and tan puppies are born very dark and the tan emerges through the black while the puppies are still nursing and the tan continues to emerge until a full adult coat.
✔ A second layer of hair, called the "undercoat," comes in around four to eight months of age. The black and tan or black and red coat will gradually lighten throughout the dog's lifetime.
✔ Another color pattern is sable. These puppies are varying shades from very dark black to a

An alert police dog keeps a look out in case he needs to join his partner.

A Black and Tan German Shepherd Dog and its Bi-color companion.

more obvious sable when born, depending upon the ultimate shade of sable in adulthood. Even the dark ones will soon display varying amounts of tan coat color under the dark hairs. It is as if the hair is dipped in black, and as you brush against the coat, the tan undercoat is seen.

✔ The German Shepherd Dog also can be solid black. This color is displayed when each parent contributes the recessive black gene to the off-spring, which results in the color black. It is more common today than 20 years ago and quite attractive.

✔ There is a color that is registered by the AKC as a bi-color, which is a color pattern that results in a dog being mostly black. The bi-color may have small tan eyebrow patches and a small amount of tan on the legs, under the tail, and underbelly. Some very dark black and tans can appear to be a bi-color pattern. The difference might be determined only by learning the color pattern of the ancestors and studying color inheritance in the German Shepherd Dog.

✔ There are also colors such as blue and liver that are displayed uncommonly and are faulted

A Sable German Shepherd Dog carries the dominant gene for sable.

The origins of the German Shepherd Dog are those of a herding dog with a desire to work.

A Black German Shepherd Dog carries two recessive genes for black.

Some breeders of the White German Shepherd Dog are seeking separate breed status.

in the AKC conformation show ring. They are genetically inherited dilutions of the strong rich colors that are preferred. Blues will have a slate gray nose but even then, those dogs may be very difficult to distinguish from their black and tan or sable counterparts. Livers are even more infrequently seen. Their coat has a brownish cast, but may also not catch the attention of an untrained eye. The character and temperament of the blue or liver dogs will not differ from other German Shepherd Dogs.

White dogs: There is quite a population of white German Shepherd Dogs in America. There are breeders who are breeding for white dogs and while the heritage of these white dogs goes

back to the original ancestors of the German Shepherd Dog, the bloodlines are different for some generations back. Some white German Shepherd Dog fanciers are seeking to have AKC separate the white dog from the colored dogs and have them recognized as a distinct breed within the AKC registration system. It is possible that this could happen in America as it has in other parts of the world. In the World Federation of Dogs (Federation Cynologique Internationale or FCI), the white German Shepherd Dog is recognized under the name Suisse Berger Blanc and as a separate breed from the German Shepherd Dog, even though they share the same original ancestry.

UNDERSTANDING GERMAN SHEPHERD DOGS

While the ear carriage, shape of the head, size of the German Shepherd Dog, and its trotting gait seem to resemble the common ancestor of all canines—the wolf—the recently completed canine genome has proven that the German Shepherd Dog and the wolf are not closely related.

Reputation

The German Shepherd Dog has the heart to serve humans and has earned our admiration and respect. The German Shepherd Dog has many excellent qualities and is admired by many for its acts of heroism. It is intelligent and high-spirited, radiates a rugged kind of strength, exhibits keen alertness, and defends its owner and his or her property with courage and tenacity. At the same time, it displays self-confidence, likes children, and is steady and unexcitable. Given appropriate upbringing, it is easy to handle and train. It loves to work and can be employed in a variety of ways— as a guard dog, police dog, working dog, or

The German Shepherd Dog is a faithful friend and companion to children.

companion dog. Each year, German Shepherd Dogs find avalanche victims and people buried under debris in disaster situations. They help police find narcotics, explosives, or concealed bodies. They find the lost, lead the blind, assist the handicapped, and are still employed as herding dogs, their original "profession."

Some people, however, are uneasy when they encounter a German Shepherd Dog. A dog with ears at attention, a look of confidence in the eyes, an alert manner, and a willingness to step out in front of its owner to assess strangers and protect, if necessary, does command respect. If the reputation of the German Shepherd Dog has suffered, it is not the dog that is at fault but the human who failed to give the dog the proper socialization and training. Nevertheless, the German Shepherd Dog

A German Shepherd Dog's keen nose enables it to smell the exterior of a car to detect the presence of narcotics.

below: Today, many German Shepherd Dogs engage in the work of herding as a sport and compete at herding trials at American Kennel Club (AKC) events.

is still one of the most popular dog breeds in the world.

A Herding Dog at Heart

If you have never seen a German Shepherd Dog engaged in its original work as a herder, try to make up for that as quickly as possible—you will be amazed! All across the United States herding fanciers have joined together for the purpose of training dogs to herd sheep and to participate in sporting events that test the abilities of the German Shepherd Dog and other herding dogs to demonstrate the sheep herding work they were bred to do. The vast majority of the herding done in the United States is done as a sport with clubs formed for that specific purpose. Each year in Germany, a national livestock herding competition is held for professional herdsmen with their German Shepherd Dogs proving their ability to work with the flocks.

The German Shepherd Dog has at heart remained a herder. The instincts are still present and while it guards the house and yard if given the opportunity, it will keep an eye on children or other pets that live in the same household and, lacking a herd of sheep to protect, may circle around its "human flock". Now and then someone will tell the story of how he or she and their guests at a lawn party were "herded" by their German Shepherd Dog. The dog managed to do this by circling the guests without their becoming aware of it until someone looked around and realized that everyone was "herded together" into one place in the yard and the dog was still happily circling the entire party, keeping its "herd" together!

A Dog That Needs Challenges

The impressive talents of the German Shepherd Dog appear to reach their highest potential especially if the dog has been carefully bred and if its owner then takes proper care of it and trains it with consistency. The dog loves to be kept busy; its intelligence, energy, and desire to work need to be properly channeled (see pages 55–61).

Depending upon the particular dog's desire for work, dogs that are "underemployed," can become a problem for their owner and their environment. The dog that wants a job and is not given one will find its own "work" to do and that work may not be compatible with the owners' expectations. The owners have no one to blame but themselves. These are the dogs whose "work" has become chewing, barking, digging, and creating a nuisance indoors or outdoors because of a lack of structured useful

The German Shepherd Dog is eager to please, and is happy being with its human doing the "work" of going for a walk and learning to heel.

activity and training. It is not the dog that is at fault, but the humans who own it and have failed to understand its needs.

History of the Breed

In the early 1900s, under the leadership of Captain Max von Stephanitz as founder and president of the German Shepherd Dog Society in Germany, the SV, the breeding of German Shepherd Dogs began a meteoric rise. By 1924 almost 50,000 dogs were listed in the studbook. The first German Shepherd Dogs came to America in the early 1900s but it was not until after World War I that the dog became popular.

After the Second World War, many of the dogs had died, and many were in the hands of the Allied Forces. Soldiers took German

The German Shepherd Dog

This is a dog of outstanding versatility. It has a keen intelligence, an extraordinary ability to be trained, and a willingness to work, while being physically strong and still agile. The German Shepherd Dog ranks as one of the most popular dog breeds in the world. The breed standard specifies a graceful gait, covering ground without wasted motion. The stiff, thick, flat, coarse hair with a thick undercoat and straight, close-fitting hair on top makes the dog adaptable to all weather conditions. The most common color is the black and tan or black and red.

The German Shepherd Dog is a very watchful guardian.

Shepherd Dogs home with them. Breeding programs in the other European countries had been disrupted. German breeders had to begin again but there were still some good dogs in the hands of conscientious breeders and within a few years, under the guidance of the SV using the breeding principles defined by Captain von Stephanitz, there were once again dogs of excellent quality in Germany. Many good dogs were imported to the United States to become part of the breeding stock and contribute to the fine quality of the German Shepherd Dog in America. In these years it was a sport for the wealthy in America and dogs imported from Germany by well-known breeders continued to exert a strong influence on the breed into the 1950s and 1960s.

The Breed Standard

The breed standard describes the way an ideal representative of a particular breed looks. The breed standard is defined in the country of origin of that breed. The standard for the German Shepherd Dog has been translated into many languages but retains the original intent of the breed standard in Germany. The national parent organization in the United States is the German Shepherd Dog Club of America, Incorporated which is a member club of the American Kennel Club. The breed standard adopted by the German Shepherd Dog Club of America, Incorporated (GSDCA) is communicated to members of the club, breeders of German Shepherd Dogs, GSDCA member clubs, and to the American Kennel Club (AKC). The AKC, in turn, communicates the standard to all AKC judges so that uniform judging criteria for the German Shepherd Dog is known to all judges, breeders, owners, and other individuals who wish to study the breed.

A breed standard and description of the way an ideal representative of the German Shepherd Dog is supposed to look follows.

German Shepherd Dog Breed Standard

General appearance: The first impression of a good German Shepherd Dog is that of a strong, agile, well muscled animal, alert and full

The natural beauty of the German Shepherd Dog attracts admirers from every walk of life.

of life. It is well balanced, with harmonious development of the forequarter and hindquarter. The dog is longer than tall, deep-bodied, and presents an outline of smooth curves rather than angles. It looks substantial and not spindly, giving the impression, both at rest and in motion, of muscular fitness and nimbleness without any look of clumsiness or soft living. The ideal dog is stamped with a look of quality and nobility—difficult to define, but unmistakable when present. Secondary sex characteristics are strongly marked, and every animal gives a definite impression of masculinity or femininity, according to its sex.

The trot is a ground covering gait that shows grace and power.

At attention, the head is raised.

Temperament: The breed has a distinct personality marked by direct and fearless, but not hostile, expression, self-confidence and a certain aloofness that does not lend itself to immediate and indiscriminate friendships. The dog must be approachable, quietly standing its ground and showing confidence and willingness to meet overtures without itself making them. It is poised, but when the occasion demands, eager and alert; both fit and willing to serve in its capacity as companion, watchdog, blind leader, herding dog, or guardian, whichever the circumstances may demand. The dog must not be timid, shrinking behind its master or handler; it should not be nervous, looking about or upward with anxious expression or showing nervous reactions, such as tucking of tail, to strange sounds or sights. Lack of confidence under any surroundings is not typical of good character. Any of the above deficiencies in character which indicate shyness must be penalized as very serious faults and any dog

This Black and Tan male has good body proportions.

exhibiting pronounced indications of these must be excused from the ring. It must be possible for the judge to observe the teeth and to determine that both testicles are descended. Any dog that attempts to bite the judge must be disqualified. The ideal dog is a working animal with an incorruptible character combined with body and gait suitable for the arduous work that constitutes its primary purpose.

The complete German Shepherd breed standard can be found on the AKC Web site or by calling the AKC and requesting a copy.

The male on the left and the female on the right display the masculine and feminine characteristics of their genders.

CHOOSING A GERMAN SHEPHERD DOG

Before you buy a German Shepherd Dog, take the time to think through all the consequences of such an acquisition. The dog is a social animal and will not be happy if it is confined and separated from the family.

Considerations

Ask yourself whether you and your family can offer the dog a good home and the proper care. You also need to be aware that the average life span of a German Shepherd Dog is 12 years. During this entire time, you are responsible for the well-being of your pet. You are making a commitment for the lifetime of the dog. The dog is a living, feeling being. It is not just another possession.

Lifestyle Questions

The following questions are intended to help you decide whether to buy a German Shepherd Dog:

1. As far as both your career and your private life are concerned, are you able to make

The potential life span of a German Shepherd Dog is 12 to 15 years.

plans over a period of about 12 years? Having a dog means that you will have to modify your habits and even your lifestyle.

2. If you do not own your home, are you allowed to keep a pet at your residence?

3. Are you going to be annoyed about having dog hair around? German Shepherd Dogs shed a lot. All dogs are social animals. The dog will not be happy isolated from the family or confined to the yard. To relegate them to existence in confinement in the yard or garage is cruel. Having a dog live with you means that you will have dog hair around your home and will be picking up and vacuuming dog hair several times a week. If this will be a problem or an annoyance, you might think about getting a breed that does not shed.

4. Do you have a fenced-in yard? Being social animals, German Shepherd Dogs are happiest living with the family but must have access to a safe, secure yard in which to eliminate.

Puppies are hard to resist. Bringing a puppy into your home is a commitment for the lifetime of the dog.

Get your puppy used to the leash early. It should walk at your left side. Talking to it in a friendly tone will encourage it to keep up with you.

5. Are you prepared to be active with your dog several times a day, even in bad weather? Regular activity with your dog is a habit you will need to develop.

6. Can you guarantee that the dog will not be left alone for long periods of time? A German Shepherd Dog can adjust to the members of the family being away for work or school during the day, but if you also regularly go out again in the evening for activities that do not include the dog, you may not have time to give a dog the attention it needs.

7. Do you have the time to teach your dog the basics, give it advanced training later on, or engage in athletic activities with it? If you are a first-time owner of a German Shepherd Dog,

German Shepherd Dogs have plenty of energy for vigorous outdoor activity.

you will need to learn how to teach your dog proper dog manners. A German Shepherd Dog will quickly learn if is owner is not "in charge" or lacks consistent expectations for proper dog behavior, and depending upon a given dog's assertiveness, a German Shepherd Dog can be quick to take advantage of this situation by being the one "taking charge."

8. Are you willing to plan your vacations so that you can take your dog along? If not, is there someone familiar to the dog who will take care of it when you are away or sick? Not all dogs can tolerate being boarded; some will go on hunger strikes and grieve when being separated from their master. You will need to plan ahead to enable your dog to make the adjustment.

9. Are you prepared to pay for your dog's food, grooming expenses, annual preventive treatments, and veterinary costs as well as a dog license and a liability insurance policy? You may want to discuss getting a dog with your insurance agent.

10. Are all the members of your family in agreement about the purchase of a German Shepherd Dog? If both partners are not committed to having a dog, it can become a serious source of friction and disagreement.

11. Does anyone in your family suffer from allergies? Individuals who are prone to allergies may not tolerate being in an environment with dogs that shed. If you are uncertain, consult with your physician before buying a dog.

Play time can also be used as a time to teach the puppy to fetch and release.

Whether you choose a male or female depends primarily on your own personal preference.

Male or Female?

Whether you acquire a male or a female depends primarily on your personal preference. In my experience, there are no significant differences in character and temperament—a male is just as affectionate as a female; females are just as naturally protective as males.

The male has a more imposing outward appearance than the female. He may be more inclined to be dominant and may get into scuffles with other males. On walks, he marks his territory with urine at every opportunity. Discuss neutering your male with the breeder and with your veterinarian. Some breeders and veterinarians believe that neutering can lessen male aggression.

The female comes into heat anywhere between six and nine months of age and you will want to plan to have her spayed before then. It has been shown that females spayed before they come into season for the first time have less incidence of breast cancer.

Puppy or Adult?

Choosing a puppy has definite advantages. You can have a direct influence on the dog's developmental phases by training it properly and fostering its potential (see Training Your Puppy, pages 47–53). While rearing the puppy, however, you need plenty of time, patience, consistency, and firmness.

Before acquiring a puppy, gather information about dog training and dog behavior. Mistakes in care and training can cause unwanted behaviors that have been unintentionally encouraged by the owners. It is important for the owners of a German Shepherd Dog to be able to "read" the body language of their dog.

With an adult dog, the process of physical development and house-training is already complete, and its character has already been molded. From these standpoints, you will have to do less work with your pet at first. Keep in mind, however, that a change of ownership, new surroundings, and unfamiliar people will require significant adjustment by the dog for up to four to six months. You will need to show plenty of understanding for your new pet in the first few weeks.

Acquiring an Adult Dog

Breeders

Experienced breeders are a good source for adult German Shepherd Dogs as well as young adults, juveniles, and puppies. Many breeders have adult dogs that they would be willing to let go to a good home if the buyer's desire for an adult dog is made known. Reputable breeders will take back an animal at any age that they have bred. Breeders may have had a dog returned as a result of a death, divorce, or loss of a job in the dog's former family. The breeder may be looking for a good pet home for this dog. He or she may have kept a dog for show that they later decided not to show and have not yet placed. These dogs can be wonderful pets.

Rescue Organizations

Rescue organizations are connected to a network of volunteer homes for dogs that have been surrendered by their owners. These volunteers are experienced dog owners and in these rescue homes the dogs undergo evaluation, training, and are assessed for their ability to be placed with a new owner. You can rely on these individuals to give you an honest assessment of the dog you are considering adopting.

Adoption of a dog is a commitment to the dog for the rest of its lifetime. Adoption of a dog or a puppy should not be embarked upon without considerable thought and a willingness to devote time to the dog and its training. Adult dogs will adjust to their new homes and the routine in time but do not be surprised if the adjustment period is as much as four to six months. A kind but firm hand and consistency in what you ask of the dog will provide the atmosphere for an adjustment as soon as can be expected.

Puppies grow quickly and their training takes time and understanding.

American or European Dog?

While within each of these styles there exist dogs with a wide range of energy level, strength of character, and willfulness, in general, the American-style dog will not have such a need to "have a job," will tend to be more laid back, and will be less apt to challenge the head of the house for the position of "top dog." If your lifestyle is not quite so active and your wish is for a companion that will play ball but also lay at your feet and watch TV with you, this might be your choice.

If you have an active lifestyle and are on the go and can involve your dog in a large part of your social life, or want a dog that enjoys work—even if this work is the participation in a sport that proves the working ability and versatility of the German Shepherd Dog—then your choice might be the European-style dog. The European-style dog and American dogs bred from performance or training lines have an energy level to maintain a strong work ethic.

In either case, prepare a list of questions, be willing to share your expectations in dog ownership, and talk to a number of breeders about their dogs before making your decision.

Finding a Breeder or Club

On the Internet

Many individuals are using the Internet to search for a dog. The best place to start is at the AKC web site at *www.akc.org*. From there you will find the Web site of the German Shepherd Dog Club of America, Inc. and to the breed rescue organizations under the Clubs page. For more information about the German Shepherd Dog from the AKC home page, select the Breed link.

✔ To find contacts for your local area you can start with a club search by clicking the Club link, then select Conformation Clubs. You can search for a specialty club in your state. The contact name for the clubs in your area will be displayed. If your state does not have a specialty club for German Shepherd Dogs, then select "All Breed" for your state and it will list the kennel clubs in your area and the contact name. You can then get a recommendation from the contact person for reputable breeders in your area.

✔ From the AKC web site home page you can also select for the online services. Then select for breeder referral then, on the next page, click the link to the National Club Breeder

TIP

Breeder Evaluation

Take special care to evaluate the breeder and the breeding management of dogs sold through an ad in the newspaper and on web sites.

✔ Check references for these sources. Puppy mills frequently advertise their puppies for sale in this way.

✔ If you buy a puppy out of pity, you are only lending support to the practice of people who unscrupulously exploit animals.

✔ Do not buy a puppy on a raffle, silent auction or e-bay. Responsible breeders want to know where their puppies are going. Being the highest bidder would not be considered qualifying criteria to determine the placement of a puppy.

Referral, which will take you to the name of the contact person for German Shepherd Dogs. From the online services page you can also click breeder classifieds, then click on Search Classified Listings.

✔ Scrolling down to the Breeder classified link on two pages and identifying the breed and area that you wish to search, you will be provided with names to select that, after clicking on Print Report, will then be displayed with breeder profiles. Be suspicious of those breeders who have not answered the questions on the breeder profiles. You will also be able to see the name of the sire and dam and whether or not the breeder has certified the hips and elbows. If the hips or elbows are certified the number will appear below the name of the dog. You will want to make other contacts in the region to check references.

Dog Shows

Dog shows are an excellent place to meet people and their German Shepherd Dogs. If you have made contacts in your area be sure to ask if there are any dog shows coming up. You can also find out when a dog show is going to be in your area from the AKC web site by clicking on Events and then on Conformation from the AKC home page. From there you would click on Superintendents.

To find dog shows in your area, you would explore the Web sites of the various superintendents. Start with MF-B and Jack Onofrio; you will find interesting information exploring the others as well. A week before the show the detailed information regarding the judging times for German Shepherd Dogs and the directions to the show site as well, will be available from the Superintendents Web site.

Clubs and Organizations

For those without Internet access there is club and contact information for the AKC and the German Shepherd Dog Club of America, Inc. provided at the back of the book.

Gather information from the American Kennel Club, the German Shepherd Dog Club of America, Inc., and the German Shepherd Dog Club of America—Working Dog Association. They can give you the addresses of breeders who are members of these clubs and adhere to strict breeding regulations. Visit as many breeders as you can so that you can compare the animals themselves as well as the conditions in which they are kept. Don't be put off by having

Dog shows are an excellent place to meet breeders and other dog owners.

to make long trips to do this. The important thing is to get a physically and mentally healthy puppy.

With small breeders, the puppies are likely to be raised in the home. They are accustomed to people and may even be well on their way to being house-trained before they leave their first homes. Puppies raised in a kennel, on the other hand, may not be as well socialized and may appear to be disinterested in having contact with people because they have had little or no experience with social interaction with humans.

The cleanliness of and the conditions in which puppies are kept will be an important factor in your selection.

Puppies raised within the breeder's home are likely to have been socialized to people and household noises.

Avoid farms or kennels that have multiple breeds. In most cases, such kennels are no more than puppy mills cared for by too few and not very knowledgeable people whose main interest is not the dogs but making money from the breeding of dogs. Search out a breeder who breeds only German Shepherd Dogs and who raises the animals in a manner suitable to this breed.

What to Look For

1. Make sure the facility is kept clean, and the breeding animals are in perfect condition and well cared for.

2. The breeder should be affectionate in his or her dealings with the dogs. The mother dog, or dam, and her puppies should display no fear of the breeder or of you.

3. The puppies should be allowed inside the breeder's house, in order to become accustomed to visitors and household noises by the time they go to new homes.

4. The breeder should ask questions about your personal circumstances and the puppy's new living conditions. This interest speaks well for the breeder; it indicates that he or she feels responsible for the puppies' future.

Do not buy under the following circumstances:

1. You are not allowed to take a look at the facilities.

2. The puppies are growing up in a cage, far from the breeder's living quarters.

3. The breeder has more than two litters or several different breeds. Such breeders have little time to pay attention to puppies during the imprinting phases. The omission of specific experiences during the critical socialization periods can lead to the development of behavioral problems that are difficult to overcome.

Papers and Pedigree

The term "papers" is a reference to an American Kennel Club document provided to the buyer that is a proof of registration of the litter with the AKC. While there are other registries in the United States, the American Kennel Club registration is the only registration that will be recognized by other countries and in turn, the AKC will recognize the registration of foreign-bred animals from other countries.

A litter can be registered with the American Kennel Club only if both the sire and dam of the litter are registered with them. The information provided on the "papers" are the litter or individual registration number, the date of birth, sex, the sire and dam, their registration numbers and any titles held by them, their hip X-ray number and status if filed with the Orthopedic Foundation of America, as well as the breeder, owner, and date the registration was issued. Individual registration papers also include information on the color of the registered animal.

A pedigree is a document listing the sire and dam and several generations of grandparents, which is provided by the breeder. A certified pedigree can be obtained from the American Kennel Club that will provide certified information including sire, dam, and additional generations of ancestry information in a standardized format including registration numbers and titles held.

Immunization

Not only are inoculations against an array of harmful or potentially fatal diseases a pivotal part of your German Shepherd Dog's preventive health plan, but in most places some of these vaccinations are also required by law!

══════ TIP ══════

Initial Veterinary Examination

Before buying the puppy, review the written contract for a provision that allows you the opportunity to have your own veterinarian examine the puppy once more before the sale is final. Most reputable breeders will provide this option for you to have a veterinary examination done at your expense within two to ten days after you take the puppy from the breeder's premises. This is an additional assurance that the puppy is in good health and provides for ongoing health care and timely administration of any additional required vaccinations that the puppy needs.

The majority of German Shepherd Dogs are Black and Tan, but all colors can be registered with the AKC.

The color black is not as frequently seen as Black and Tan or Sable.

Your puppy may have had its first immunizations at about six weeks of age while still at the breeder's. These initial shots were vaccinations for distemper and measles and possibly for parvovirus, canine hepatitis, leptospirosis, parainfluenza, coronavirus, and bordetella (see Preventive Care and Diseases, beginning on page 77).

The vaccination record should be a part of the permanent paperwork you obtain when you purchase a puppy or an adult dog. Your pet's veterinarian needs to know what vaccinations (or other treatments) your dog received before you became its owner. This complete account-

CHECKLIST

Information on Contract of Sale

✔ Your name, address, and telephone number as well as those of the breeder.

✔ The puppy's name, sex, date of birth, AKC litter or individual registration number, the sire and dam of the puppy and their AKC registration numbers.

✔ The price paid for the puppy.

✔ The date the puppy changed hands.

✔ Any conditions of the sale such as spay, neuter, and limited registration, which provides that any offspring resulting from this animal, will not be registered.

✔ If the animal is sold as a show dog, the contract should specify the guarantees and remedies in place should the animal not be of show quality as an adult. The reasons for an animal not being of show quality can vary considerably depending upon the age of the animal when purchased. A missing molar tooth is an example. This would not be known at nine weeks of age but would eliminate a puppy as a show quality adult because the German Shepherd Dog standard specifies a missing molar as a serious fault.

✔ The refund due to the buyer if the buyer returns the puppy for health reasons following the examination by a veterinarian.

✔ If there are any guarantees for hip dysplasia, the specific level of the guarantee, through what age the guarantee is applied, whether or not the dog must be returned to the breeder, and the adjustment that is provided.

ing of what has been done to and for your dog will form the foundation of your pet's health records, which should be kept current and accurate throughout the life of the dog.

Usually, the breeder will have wormed the puppies before selling them (see page 80). Ask how often and with what preparations the puppy was wormed.

The Contract of Sale

When you buy a dog, it is essential to conclude your purchase with a written contract of sale. The breeder should give you this. It provides both the buyer and the seller with legal safeguards. If legal disputes arise, the contract of sale will be useful. It should contain the information found in the Checklist on page 28.

Choosing a Puppy

Puppies between eight and ten weeks old are the easiest to get settled in new surroundings, and you can get an early start on training during the socialization phase (Training Your Puppy, pages 47–50). Several weeks before the puppies will be ready to go to new homes, get acquainted with them at the breeder's, then visit them on a frequent basis to observe them for extended periods at play and at mealtimes. A reputable breeder will welcome your interest and help you pick out a puppy. He or she can tell you which dog has the particular traits you are looking for. You yourself can check the state of the puppy's health by noting the following:

✔ A healthy puppy is lively and playful.
✔ It is well nourished (neither too fat nor too thin).
✔ It comes up to you inquisitively and trustingly.

Healthy puppies are active and playful.

✔ Its coat is clean and glossy; it should not smell of feces or urine.
✔ Its eyes and nose are free of discharge; its ears are clean.

Before pick-up day, do the following:
✔ A few days ahead of time, bring a blanket to the breeder, so that it will pick up the smell of the kennel. It will make the puppy's separation from its mother and siblings easier and help it feel at home in its new surroundings.
✔ Ask the breeder what the puppy is being fed, since it usually will react to abrupt changes in its diet by developing gastrointestinal upsets.
✔ Make an appointment with the veterinarian to have your new pet thoroughly examined.

Accommodations for Your Dog

Taking proper care of a dog also means that the dog spends its time where its "people" live.

Indoor sleeping place: The dog needs a dry, draft-free spot in your home, a place from which it has an adequate overview of its "family." It can retreat to that spot whenever it

The ears on an adult should be erect and firm, but the ears on a puppy begin to come up between two and four months of age, and they may go up and down during that time, until teething is over.

wants peace and quiet and should not be disturbed by children at such times. Provide a crate to which the puppy can retreat (see the section on crate training on page 39). You can also give the dog a soft, washable blanket to lie on. Be careful to observe if your puppy is going to be a blanket chewer. If the puppy begins to chew holes in the blanket, take it away and substitute newspaper. Or, you can spray fabrics with bitter-tasting substances that are not toxic but discourage chewing, such as Bitter Apple or Bitter Orange, which are available at pet stores. Puppies that habitually consume fabrics are at risk for getting an intestinal upset or even intestinal obstruction following ingestion of fabric. You may wish to start with newspaper and try a blanket at an older age when the puppy has outgrown the desire to chew on fabrics.

══ TIP ══

Puppy-proofing

• Survey your home for hazards such as exposed electrical cords, chemicals under the sink, ant bait in the yard, or hazards in other areas where the puppy will be exposed to them. Puppy-proof your home by eliminating these hazards, as you would do for a human toddler.
• If you have treasured knickknacks you will want to be sure that they are put away.
• If you leave aspirin or prescription drugs out on the kitchen table where they can easily be knocked on the floor or where a puppy can reach them when climbing on a chair, you will want to put them where a curious puppy can't get at them.
• Things left out and accessible to the puppy, even shoes on the floor, are at risk for a puppy exploring its new surroundings.
• Purchase a kennel, other essential equipment, and chew toys from a pet store.

Shoes are not a suitable toy. A puppy will not be able to distinguish between your favorite shoes and "toy shoes."

A dog is a social animal and it is unsuitable to keep a puppy isolated from its family by being confined in the yard or garage. It is cruel to keep a social pack animal confined and the puppy will not be happy there.

The outdoors: You will want to have fencing around your yard to keep your dog safe when it is outside. You will find that house-training is best facilitated by having the puppy inside exclusively and by accompanying the puppy when it goes out to eliminate. You may want to have an area within your yard designated for the purpose of having the dog eliminate in that area.

Important: Keeping any dog chained is inappropriate, even if the chain is long and allows the dog to move around. Chaining a dog stimulates aggression and other unwanted behavior.

Essential Equipment

Before you bring your puppy home, you should have all its equipment and accessories ready.

Collar: The collar for your new puppy should be adjustable and designed to grow along with your pet. Simple collars made of leather or nylon are ideal; you may have to purchase several before your puppy is full grown. For adult dogs, collars made of soft leather or soft but heavy synthetic fabrics are tried-and-true choices. Chain collars should be used only for training situations or when the dog is being walked. Chain collars easily catch on objects

It is not difficult to teach your dog to use a specific place for elimination.

and dogs have harmed themselves by being choked after having gotten caught on a knob or hook. The ring of the collar can catch on a pail handle or get caught by dropping through a grate or vent—even in a crate—and the dog will harm itself by struggling violently against it in an attempt to get free. These chain collars are designed to tighten up and do not always release the chokehold it has on your dog.

Dog identification: In case your pet should ever get lost, you should purchase and identification tag to place on the dog's collar. A microchip, a tiny cylindrical chip placed by a veterinarian under the skin of a dog, is a permanent method of identification. All shelters now have microchip readers and this provides a sure way to have your lost pet returned to you if you follow through and register the microchip number with the American Kennel Club Companion Animal Recovery (see more information on page 92).

Leash: The leash for the puppy should be made of leather, approximately 6 feet (1.8 m) in length and equipped with a secure snap hook. Chain-link leashes are not suitable. They hurt your hands and represent a safety hazard to the puppy. A handy innovation is a spring-loaded retractable nylon leash that is approximately 20 feet (6 m) long. When on a stroll and not under commands, it allows the puppy to go out to investigate the environment and come back to you without you or the puppy getting tangled in the leash.

Balls to chase and things to toss make good dog toys.

Coat and nail care: Buy a brush with fine teeth called a slicker brush, a shedding comb, and a dog comb with widely spaced teeth and one with more closely spaced teeth. You will need a toenail clipper as well (see Grooming on pages 74–75).

Food and water dishes: These have to be sturdy, skidproof, and easy to clean. I recommend the practical bowls made of stainless steel. Holders made of wood can be made or purchased to hold the bowls to keep them from skidding while the dog is eating and elevated for ease of reaching. For water you can use a small pail, or a deep stainless steel dish. Ceramic bowls are acceptable but not as easy to put in the dishwasher. They are also breakable and some dogs will pick up their food dishes and carry them around.

Toys: In order to keep your dog occupied and to give it something to chew on, toys are essential. Pet stores have a large assortment available. The toy should not be capable of injuring the dog, nor should it be made of a material that will splinter. Old shoes are not suitable, because the dog cannot distinguish between an old and a new shoe! Don't use rocks or small sticks. Rocks will damage the dog's teeth and small sticks might get caught on the roof of its mouth or between its teeth and cause injury. You can throw a tennis ball or a hard rubber ball to foster your pet's instinct to chase and retrieve. Play activity will be important in subsequent training. Some dogs left to play with tennis balls by themselves will crack the tennis ball and chew it up. This can be a hazard if the dog swallows pieces of tennis ball that can block the intestines and cause an intestinal obstruction, which is a medical emergency. There are balls that are sturdier than tennis balls available from pet food stores.

Dried pieces of rawhide are appealing chew toys for some dogs. If you choose to use rawhide chew toys, you will want to observe carefully what your dog does with it. Some dogs are content to gnaw on them for long periods but others chew the rawhide into chunks that they consume and later "upchuck." If your dog is one of those, you will want to withhold rawhide as a chew object as it can become a source of gastrointestinal irritation and repeated illness. There are commercially made chewable toys, such as Nylabones, that can be purchased. These chew toys come in various shapes, are hard, and provide hours of satisfying gnawing for a dog. The dog will not be able to chew pieces from them large enough to cause digestive or intestinal problems.

While your dog shouldn't sit at your table, it should have a specific and consistent place where it is fed.

ACCLIMATION AND DAILY ROUTINE

The time has come! You can pick up your puppy at the breeder's. Make an appointment, since the breeder will want to prepare for the puppy's transfer. Bring a towel along as some puppies may experience carsickness and drool during the car ride, even if they do not throw up.

Making Your Home Safe

Even before you bring your puppy home, be aware of possible dangers in your home and take steps to correct or eliminate them. Some of the things to consider as hazards are electrical cords, lamp cords, and soap and other chemicals that are kept under the sink.

The Trip Home

It is best to bring your puppy home in a car, and to have a second person accompany you. Take along a towel, a roll of paper towels, a collar, a leash, a bowl, fresh water, and some dry food. Put the puppy's collar on it, then set it on

Prepare for your puppy before you bring it home.

the floor of the car, just in front of the passenger seat, on top of the blanket you gave the breeder ahead of time. During the trip, do not let the dog have an opportunity to look out of the window. The sight of the landscape "flying by" can nauseate it. You should sit on the passenger seat, to calm the puppy down, if necessary.

On longer car trips you need to take a short break every hour or so in order to let the dog run around—on leash—so it has a chance to do its business and to get some exercise. Then give it fresh water to drink and a small amount of the dry food to eat.

The First Hours at Home

Everything is strange and new to the little puppy, and after the great excitement of the

Dangers in Your Home and Yard

Source of Danger	Possible Consequences	How to Prevent
Smooth or slippery floors	Broken bones or other injuries	Don't let dog romp around unsupervised.
Sharp or pointed objects	Cuts, puncture wounds	Don't leave dangerous objects lying around.
Indigestible children's toys	Swallowing them can lead to intestinal obstructions.	Don't leave small toys lying around.
Circuit lines, wall sockets	Electric shock (can be fatal)	Unplug cords; block wall sockets with childproof devices.
Chemicals, detergents, cleaning agents, pesticides	Poisoning, acid burns	Store out of the dog's reach; do not use chemical pesticides in your home and yard.
Poisonous house plants and outdoor plants, berries	Poisoning	Do not keep poisonous plants, or put them out of harm's way. Young dogs are particularly at risk. Do not use rat poison, insecticides, ant bait, snail bait, or weed killers.
Steep or open stairs	Danger of falling	Use a barrier to deny young dog access (childproof gate).
Balcony/deck	Danger of falling	Attach safety barrier or additional fencing (special gates available in pet stores).
Low window railings	Danger of falling	Open window only from the top; never let dog near an open window unsupervised.
Swimming pool, garden pond	Drowning	Put up safety fence; cover pool with netting; put climbing aids in garden pond; supervise dog when outdoors.
Low fence around yard	Dog may escape.	An escape-proof fence for a German Shepherd Dog has to be at least 72 inches (180 cm) high, with safeguards at the bottom to keep the dog from digging underneath it to get out.

TIP

Your Bed

If you take the puppy into your own bed out of sympathy, it will want to do so from then on, even as a full-grown dog, and by then it will weigh 60 to 80 pounds (27–36 kg)!

A place of its own and a chew toy will help a puppy to adjust to its new home.

trip, it needs peace and quiet. The other members of the family should not immediately make a beeline for the new arrival. Ask friends and relatives who also want to admire the puppy to be patient and to wait a day before visiting.

Careful acclimation: Carry the puppy, along with its blanket, to the place you have designated for it. Set out water and the puppy's customary food. After it has eaten, take it outside, so that it can answer nature's call. Then let it run around indoors and get its bearings. When it lies down, exhausted, carry it back to its blanket and let it sleep.

Choosing a name: By the time the puppy arrives, you should have settled on a name for it. Always use its name in connection with something positive—while you are petting it, for example. Then it will quickly react to its name.

The First Nights at Home

Dogs adjust well to sleeping where the rest of the family, which is now their "pack," sleeps. They are happy to sleep in the bedroom or just outside the bedroom where they can keep an eye out for everyone. Put the puppy, with its blanket, into the crate next to your bed, or you

can sleep for a few nights in the room in which you want it to stay. That way you can talk to it reassuringly when it whimpers because it misses its mother and littermates, or you can quickly carry it outside when it is restless and has to "go." During the first few weeks, you will need to get up at night to take your puppy outdoors, as its bladder is still too small to make it through the entire night.

House-training

It is important to establish an elimination routine. Initially, it is the owner who is "trained" to observe signs that the puppy needs to eliminate. When you notice your puppy displaying restlessness or sniffing or circling behavior, that

Sniffing and circling behavior precedes elimination.

is a clue that the dog needs to eliminate. In the early training it is urgent that you respond to these clues immediately. If the puppy starts to "piddle" in an inappropriate spot, simply say *"No,"* pick up the puppy and take him outside. Eventually, the signals that the puppy displays are more obvious, which allows some additional time for the owner to react and respond by letting the dog out. In general, elimination will precede and follow play and eating. Always allow the opportunity for the puppy to "piddle" the very first thing when it gets up in the morning, when awakening from naps, before and after eating, and before and after play. The puppy will usually have a bowel movement in the morning right after eating and again in the afternoon—sometimes before eating—depending upon the amount of exercise it has had. It may or may not have a bowel movement before bedtime.

Submissive Urination

Differentiate between house-training problems and submissive urination. Be aware that many German Shepherd Dog puppies will urinate a tiny bit when someone greets them or bends over to pet them. This is called "submissive urination." The way the puppy sees it, you

are bigger than they are and you just leaned over them, which is an act of dominance. In human behavior and communication, submissive urination should be thought of "as if someone gave you a bouquet of roses." Puppies will often defer to older dogs in this manner as an act of submission. When they do this to their human packmates they are saying things like, "I like you." and "You sure can be in charge!" or "What is it you would like me to do?"

Submissive urination is canine communication and in a dog pack it lets the older more dominant dogs know that the puppy does not want to challenge their position, that the puppy wants affection and acceptance, and that they are actively submissive to the top dog. The best way to extinguish submissive urination is to ignore it. You can also modify your posture when greeting a puppy that urinates submissively by squatting down to greet it. This diminishes your size and keeps you from having to lean over the puppy. This may speed up the process of extinguishing the submissive urination behavior. Many people make a mistake in disciplining the puppy for this urination, which just compounds the problem. The puppy will "piddle" even more because, in its own language and way of communicating, it is already saying, "I want to please you!" When the piddling is followed by discipline, the puppy gets confused because it doesn't understand why it

The Crate

Using a crate will facilitate house-training at your home. Use the crate overnight, as dogs do not like to soil their bed and will whimper to avoid it—this is very important. During its adjustment, the puppy may just want to be out of its crate when it awakens overnight, but you must give it an opportunity to go out to eliminate, "just in case." This will establish the routine of cleanliness in the house. Being inattentive or putting off the puppy's needs will lead to delayed house-training because it will not be able to depend upon being let out in a timely way. Bad habits are harder to break than just investing the time to establish a pattern for routine elimination behavior.

is being disciplined for "gifting you" with its submission and desire to please.

Crate training is a must.

Crate Training

If your puppy was not acquainted with being in a crate where it was raised, you will want to train your puppy to use it. Crate training can be made easier by the use of a "crate only" toy (such as a Gummybones or chew hooves) that it usually doesn't have when it is out of its crate. Additionally, a treat offered by tossing it into the crate is an easy way to get the puppy to go into the crate, then you can simply close the door. Both of these things will have your puppy looking forward to "crate time." My dogs know that when the treats come out they are going to their crates and they are there before I can even call them to "crate up." A crate offers a safe haven for the puppy while the puppy is too young and inexperienced to stay out of harm's way when it cannot be under close supervision.

Tips for Using the Crate

✔ Use the crate anytime that you are away from home or during those times when you will not be able to supervise the puppy's activity.

✔ The puppy will whine if it is in its crate and needs to eliminate.

✔ If you are still in the house in the daytime while it is crated, you will need to learn to distinguish between the puppy's real needs and simple boredom with being in its crate. Having your puppy eliminate before placing it in the crate will help you to know whether or not it just wants out to play.

✔ When you are ready to let the puppy out of its crate establish a routine of taking it immediately from the crate to outside until you are sure of the puppy's elimination routines.

Quiet spot: Neither you nor your dog should view the use of the crate as a tool for punishment. The crate is a safe, comfortable spot for the dog. It is a place that it can retreat to when it wants to rest or just get away from the activity. Your dog will view the crate as its home in the home. We like to keep the crate in our bedroom, a place away from all the activity during the day if our dog wants to retreat, and it is a comfort to the dog to be close to its humans overnight.

Size: The size of the crate should match the size of the dog. In the case of a growing puppy, it is best if you can initially acquire a crate that is comfortable for the puppy to stand up in and turn around easily, but yet not too large. If your circle of friends includes dog owners, try to borrow one of an appropriate size for this period. A crate that is too large might encourage a puppy to soil one end of it and sleep on the other end. When the puppy outgrows the smaller crate then it is time to purchase one for its adult years. A 36 × 24 × 26-inch-high (91 × 61 × 66-cm) crate will be comfortable for a small

Some dogs develop a habit of eating string toys, and tennis balls, which can cause serious digestive problems.

female of 60 pounds (27 kg) and approximately 22 inches (56 cm) at the wither. A 40 × 26 × 30-inch-high (101 × 66 × 76-cm) crate will be appropriate for a large female or an average size male of about 80 pounds (36 kg) and 26 inches (66 cm) at the wither. There are extra large crates that are 48 × 32 × 35-inches-high (122 × 81 × 89-cm) for the large males exceeding 100 pounds (45 kg) and 28 or 30 inches (71 or 76 cm) at the wither.

Toys

It is a good idea to have a variety of toys to rotate. The puppy and even adult dogs should not have access to all of the toys all of the time—rotating them provides some interesting variety and prevents boredom with the toys. Select safe toys that the dog does not choose to consume, unless they are edible toys such as Nylabones and chew hooves. Some dogs will consume fabric toys, which may pose a risk for stomach or bowel irritation or blockage. Be alert to possible problems when selecting rawhide toys. Some dogs develop infections or intolerance to rawhides and develop crusting sores on their lips. Some dogs will consume pieces that are large enough to irritate the stomach and cause them to throw up chunks of rawhide. The lip sores may resolve by themselves if caught early but may need treatment with antibiotics. Be alert to this possibility. You may wish to avoid rawhide toys in dogs with this problem. Dogs that begin to swallow large pieces generally will continue to do so; you may have to eliminate rawhides as a toy if this is the case. Puppies do not have much trouble with rawhides until they begin to get adult teeth (5–6 months). You will need to observe carefully during that time.

Puppy Development

The first eight weeks: The imprinting phases begin at the age of about two to three weeks. The puppy learns its first lessons in social behavior from its mother and littermates; then it has to imprint to humans as well. A good breeder will promote extensive contact with the puppies at this time. A puppy is too young to leave its mother and littermates before the seventh week when its nervous system is mature enough to make the separation and it can begin to learn independently.

The eighth week is the "fear imprinting" week. If the puppy has not gone to its new home during the seventh week it is best to wait until the ninth week. There should be no new experiences introduced to the puppy during this critical eighth week. It is a mistake to expose the puppy during the eighth week to the veterinary clinic. There it can be exposed to larger unfamiliar dogs and unpleasant experiences that will cause a lifetime imprinting of fear of those things. I have witnessed an otherwise happy, normal eight-week-old puppy yelping in fear, having been exposed to a large unfamiliar dog that was just curious about the newcomer and wanted to "check the puppy out." This puppy took over a year to get over strange larger dogs approaching it and during that time was anxious and cried out loudly in fear every time it was exposed to strange dogs. This could and should have been avoided.

Puppies learn proper social behavior and "dog language" from their mothers.

Ninth to twelfth weeks: During this socialization phase the puppies learn to respect the authority of the adult dogs and the rules that apply in the pack. Your puppy will now view you and your family as its "pack." It will test you to see how far it can go. Playing together is very important. It reinforces the bond between owner and pet. For these reasons, the "alpha" or "boss" male or female, in particular, needs to set aside some time each day for the puppy. The puppy also needs to play with other dogs, however, to learn canine social behavior. Some dog clubs, training schools, and other organizations offer puppy socialization, which are play sessions for that purpose (see pages 24–25).

Twelfth to twentieth weeks: During this time, the puppy is growing into a young dog. This is the most important, as well as the most vulnerable, phase in the dog's life, so far as the development of its bond to its human owner and its social behavior toward other dogs are concerned. Everything the dog experiences at this stage, whether positive or negative, becomes deeply rooted in its life. Whatever situations your pet fails to experience because you lack time for it cannot be derived from later experience. There is no way to recapture the opportunities to expose your puppy to the experiences of meeting new people, meeting and playing with other dogs, and learning that there are other physical environments such as parks, other homes, shopping centers, dog clubs, dog shows, and training centers.

From six to twelve months: The phases that will decisively influence the rest of your dog's life are now behind it. Before your pet is an adult-sized dog—that is at the age of about one year—you still have to weather its "teens," a stage at which it will challenge quite a few of

your rules. By remaining firm and consistent, however, you will get over this hurdle as well. Some dogs will experience a transient uncertainty at some time between eight and eleven months of age. They will balk at doing some things that they have readily done before and may show hesitation at some new experience. If you encounter this behavior, it is best not to force the issue. Simply and in a matter-of-fact way, take a "time-out" and return the dog to a place it considers safe, such as to its crate, the car, or home. You should wait to try that new experience another time.

The two-year-old: Somewhere around the age of two your German Shepherd Dog will begin to demonstrate its adult territorial behaviors. Without training or encouragement on your part, your dog will become protective of its family, its home, and its environment. Whatever environment your dog considers its "territory" will be considered worthy of protecting. The dog will bark at the doorbell or at unusual sounds in the night. If you want your dog to alert you to these things, you will need to pay attention to its attempts to do so, even when it is inconvenient. During the day it is easy enough to say, "Let's go see who is at the door" and accompany the dog to the door to investigate. Barking overnight will disturb your sleep, but if you command *"Quiet!"* instead of going to investigate, you will be inadvertently training your dog to think that when you are in bed,

Teaching sit *in your home can be easily accomplished when you get your puppy's attention with a treat at the same time that you say* "sit." *Raise the treat above the puppy's head so that it will sit in order to look up and see the treat.*

Adult German Shepherd Dogs are naturally protective of territory that they consider theirs.

you are not to be disturbed. By going to investigate, you teach your dog to discriminate between sounds that can be ignored and those that should raise the alarm.

Building Trust

If you and your pet are to live together in harmony, it is essential that the dog come to trust you. Without your pet's trust, you can neither teach it the fundamentals of obedience, give it advanced training later, nor engage in athletic activities with it. You must never jeopardize this relationship of trust by inconsistent behavior, use of improper force, or an outburst of temper. Don't attempt to train your dog when you are impatient or in a bad mood. Your

behavior needs to be predictable. Always use the same voice signals to tell your pet what you want of it or what is off-limits. Don't let it get away with behavior one day that you punish it for the next. Achieve your objectives patiently; otherwise, the puppy will take advantage of your inconsistency.

Trust in its environment: Slowly begin to build the puppy's trust in the world around it. During the first few weeks, don't make long excursions to unfamiliar surroundings. First explore the immediate vicinity of your home, step by step, with your pet safely on its 6-foot (2-m) puppy leash. If your puppy becomes fearful in some situation, don't change course, and don't pick it up and hold it—but don't use force either. Your pet has to be gently taught to overcome its

Teaching a dog proper manners and tricks, such as "shake," in a consistent way creates a bond and builds trust.

fear. Focus on the "scary object," kneel down, and talk soothingly to the puppy. With time, its natural curiosity will win out. A treat offered as a reward will help calm the puppy. Let your pet establish friendly contact with people and other animals. This is critical for its socialization, and it will not undermine subsequent instincts as a guardian of home and family.

Physical Contact

Many of the dogs that are brought to behaviorists because of problems with their training or their overall behavior are suffering from a common difficulty: Their owners are unable to establish physical contact with them. Intimate partnership between a dog and its owner is a prerequisite for problem-free pet ownership. Starting with physical contact with its littermates, and later with humans, a young dog gradually acquires better control of its movements. In addition, as its "body awareness"

develops, its confidence is bolstered and it becomes fully capable of realizing its physical and mental potential. Humans benefit from physical contact with pets as well: Studies have shown that spending a great deal of time in activities with a pet lowers high blood pressure, slows the pulse, and dissipates stress.

Communication

Dogs communicate by means of their body language and vocalizations, the roots of which lie deep in their past, in their genetic heritage. Through body language or vocalization, the dog tells you what is important to it at the moment. Dogs do not have an abstract concept of time. It is not what was or what will be that matters but only the *"now."* You will need to keep this in mind when you are trying to influence your pet. Naturally, young and adult dogs have a better command of "language" than puppies, which first have to practice all the forms of behavior within their pack by playing with their littermates.

Body Language

You will not understand your dog if you pay attention only to isolated signals, such as a wagging tail or laid-back ears. All the body signals given by the dog are meant to be interpreted as a whole; only then will you understand what your pet wants or how it feels at the moment.

Body language is innate. Observance of the dog rules of body language is possible, however, only if the dog had a chance to practice them repeatedly in its imprinting phases with its littermates especially until it is seven weeks old. It is important, again through puppy socialization with other puppies in formal or informal settings from nine weeks until its twentieth week (see pages 41–42). If you fail to offer a dog this opportunity in very early puppyhood, later on you will have a German Shepherd Dog that cannot adhere to the canine social rules. That may make it antisocial or even dog-aggressive to other dogs, which could be a hazard to you and to other dogs when confronting them in public situations such as passing them on the street or in a park. Smaller dogs could be hurt by a German Shepherd Dog and conversely, your dog can be injured itself it if runs across a stronger dog and fails to defer to it. It is important for you to learn the meaning of the following body language:

Trying to impress: The dog walks stiff-legged to make itself seem larger. Its eyes are averted, its ears point to the front, and its tail is raised high in the air and waves slightly. Males sometimes turn one side to the other dog or try to impress it by "riding" it. Efforts to intimidate also include marking with urine, followed by digging and scraping with its hind legs.

Threatening to attack: Here the dog lowers its head slightly, but fixes its eyes on its opponent. Its lips are drawn back, and its ears point to the rear. By fully extending its limbs, it tries to look bigger. It may also bristle its hair to look bigger and to signal aggression. Its tail is raised up over its back. Caution is now in order, since the dog is about to bite.

Passive submission: The weaker dog displays passive submission as early as the intimidation phase or, at the latest, during the threat phase, by avoiding eye contact, throwing itself down

Body Contact Exercises

Touch your dog deliberately and consciously, but do not massage it. Working on muscles more intensely might become unpleasant for the dog and do more harm than good. Note the following:
- The exercises should always last for several minutes.
- Pressing gently, make circular motions with your palms and fingertips, so that only the skin over the muscles is moved.
- Start on the dog's abdomen, moving your hands rapidly at first, then more slowly, slowing your breathing at the same time.
- As you work, talk to your pet or hum soothingly, in a deep voice.
- Once the dog is relaxed, let one hand lie still on its body while you continue to work on its entire body systematically, making small circular movements with your other hand.
- If your dog enjoys these few minutes of touching, then you can proceed to more sensitive parts of its body.

Carefully work on the skin between its toes and the pads of its feet. Run your index finger and thumb over each ear, moving from the base of the ear to the tip. You can experiment with other areas as well, as your dog gets increasingly used to being touched.

Daily, purposeful physical contact will be beneficial for the dog and establish a partnership between dog and owner.

Dogs communicate using canine body language. Dominance, submission, and play are learned in social interaction with other dogs.

on its back, pointing its ears to the rear, and simultaneously drawing its lips into a "grin." Its tail is tucked between its legs. On some occasions, however, the dog makes licking motions, whimpers, whines, or cries out. Sometimes it also submissively urinates.

This gesture of lying on its back as a sign of submissiveness causes the stronger dog to leave its opponent alone. Even puppies instinctively use this defensive measure—they lie on their back when faced by adult dogs.

Active submission: The dog's eyes are trustingly and attentively focused on you, and its body and tail are in relaxed positions.

Invitation to play: The dog flattens its forequarters on the ground, looks at you alertly, and raises its hindquarters high in the air, with tail wagging. It alternates between this position and frisky little jumps in the air, moving around

TIP

Attacking

Dogs have been known to attack without a preliminary warning, immediately after their effort to intimidate. Conversely, a dog also may attack without first trying to intimidate an opponent.

you in a circle. It behaves the same way when inviting another dog to play.

Vocalizations

Dogs have a wide range of vocalizations at their command. Even while being nursed, little puppies make "growls" of satisfaction.

Barking: An adult dog barks in a variety of timbres on many different occasions: to warn about strange dogs and animals, to express great joy, or to issue an invitation to play. Sometimes the dog merely "woofs" with closed mouth and slightly inflated cheeks, such as when it is excited by something it cannot yet identify. As a rule, the German Shepherd Dog has a moderate inclination to bark, and you can encourage or discourage this tendency through training.

Growling: Dogs are able to growl from the second week of life onward. They make this noise later as well, both in play and in earnest, in offensive or defensive situations.

Whimpering: The dog can express submissiveness in this way. It also lends emphasis when the dog is begging for food or asking someone to play. In addition, a dog whimpers when it is in pain. When puppies express their uneasiness or discomfort, they whimper or whine.

Howling: If a dog is left home alone, it often will follow a short period of barking with long, drawn-out howling. Some dogs howl when they are exposed to high-frequency tones.

Yipping and squealing: Both are signs of pain or anxiety, particularly in puppies.

Training Your Puppy

Your puppy's training begins the very day it enters its new home. Training procedures for dogs over six months old are described on HOW-TO pages 52–53.

Training Rules

✔ Training is based on the dog's trust in its owner. The trainer has to be consistent and patient.

✔ *Roughness and hitting are taboo!* After a successful drill, lavish your pet with praise. You want it to feel that it is being allowed to do something *with* you, not that it *has* to do it.

✔ Training is not limited to a daily hour of practice or a training course that meets weekly. There you will receive only guidelines that you have to put into effect repeatedly during the rest of the week.

✔ With a puppy, always squat or crouch when you start an exercise.

✔ Use body language and facial expressions as you work. The dog will be watching you very closely.

✔ When giving commands, the most important thing is the tone of your voice, not its volume.

✔ Always give short commands, using your pet's name; for example: *"Arco! Sit!"* Long sentences will confuse the dog.

✔ During all the initial exercises, your pet should be hungry, so motivate it with treats.

Reward the dog with a treat when teaching a quick response to the sit command.

Never initiate strenuous physical exercise or play after your dog has been fed, as there is a danger of gastric torsion or stomach upset.

✔ With all exercises, take a break to play after a few minutes have passed.

"No" or "Out"

It is essential to decide on a word or sound that will cause your dog to stop immediately what it is doing. Many owners choose the word *"No"* or *"Out"* for this purpose. I have found that I use the words *"No"* and *"Out"* in many other contexts, and have found that a very nasal sound *"Aaungh"* or *"Aauck"* is more effective in communicating the "stop what you are doing" command. I have even had "guest dogs" that have spent a weekend with my dogs and have caught on to what this means before the day is out. Whatever command you choose should be used consistently to stop the dog from whatever it is doing. This is known as putting something under taboo. Utter these commands in a threatening tone of voice. If that doesn't help take hold of the coat on the nape of the puppy's neck to scold it. It is all right if the puppy gives a cry of fear. You can be certain that it will repeatedly test your ability to remain consistent. If you give in you will have lost the battle for good.

Taking something out of its mouth: Place one hand firmly around the dog's muzzle from above. With your fingers, press its lips (flews) firmly against its teeth, saying *"Out!"* in a threatening voice until it lets go of the object. Then praise your pet and reward it with a treat. Do not let your puppy mouth your hands; substitute a toy.

Leash Training

Collar (see Essential Equipment, pages 31–32): Get your puppy accustomed to its collar by first having it wear the collar indoors.

Leash (see page 32): The leash is your "telephone line" to the dog, through which you can control it. Hold the leash in your right hand, while the puppy walks at your left. Do not put your hand through the loop of the leash. Many people have gotten broken bones and serious

Taking the puppy by the scruff to reinforce discipline if **"no"** *or* **"aaungh"** *or* **"out"** *is insufficient.*

scrapes when their dogs suddenly ran to something and they were pulled into an object or pulled over onto the sidewalk or pavement because they could not let go of the leash or pull back on it effectively. First it has to learn to estimate the area defined by its approximately 6-foot (1.8-m) leash. Before it has a chance to pull the line taut and tug at it, give the leash a short jerk—depending on your pet's degree of stubbornness—and say *"No"* at the same time. Then relax the tension on the leash immediately. With the leash in this slack, but controlled position, you can take the dog for a walk to relieve itself, once it is past puppyhood.

The Come Command

In fenced-in areas, you can let the puppy run loose, off the leash. Here you need to take advantage of the dog's pack instincts and show it that it should not go more than about 10 feet (3–5 m) away from you. If, from that distance, it does not respond to your calling its name or giving the *come* command by immediately running toward you, react either by hiding or by walking off in the opposite direction. Your puppy will soon come bounding after you. Praise it or reward it with a little treat.

Important: Never run after the dog. Don't keep announcing your location by calling your pet's name; otherwise, it will always know where you are and will see no reason to come.

"Sit" and "Release"

To teach your pet these commands, as well as the *down* and *stand* exercises (see pages 52–53), use a sturdy leather or plastic collar and a leather leash about 3 feet (1 m) long.

How to proceed: The puppy, on leash, should stand at your left side. In your right hand, hold the leash and a treat, which you hold over its head so that it has to look upward to see it. Give the *sit* command and call your pet by name. At the same time, gently push down on its hindquarters with your left hand. When it is seated, give it the treat and praise it. After a few seconds, give the *release* command and let it race around and play with you. Practice regularly, until the exercise works with the *sit* command alone.

The Stay Command

Introduce the *stay* command once the dog is reliably sitting for a full minute with you standing next to it. The *stay* command is introduced by saying the word *"Stay"* firmly and placing your open hand in front of the dog's eyes like a "stop traffic sign" in a *hand* command. Move your hand to your side, slowly extend your right foot one step and bring your left foot up even with it. Repeat the *stay* and the *stop* hand command if the dog looks as though it is going to move. After a brief moment, take a step back so you are where you started before you release the dog with a specific word that your dog will associate with finishing the exercise, such as "Okay" or "Free." Reward the dog with a treat or toss the ball a couple of times, and repeat the exercise. Gradually increase the number of steps forward and backward, going around the dog, until the dog remains in the *sit–stay* as you walk all the way around it. Only release the dog from your original starting position. Once the dog reliably stays when you are close to it on a single *stay* command, you can begin to gradually increase your distance away from your dog on a single *stay* command. Repeat the *stay* command as often as you need to during the teaching phase, but do not increase your dis-

Stay is commanded at the same time that the left hand is placed in front of the dog's eyes as a "stop sign." The dog learns the hand signal for stay as the word "stay" is uttered simultaneously with the reinforcing hand signal.

tance until your dog is reliable at the distance you are working on.

Living Together

Through consistent and appropriate training and proper care, the dog will find its subordinate position of rank within its human/dog pack, and that will allow it to become a well-balanced member of the family. The human members of the pack will need to take a leadership role and provide training. An assertive, headstrong dog, in a household where strong human leadership is lacking and where no one has undertaken the training of the dog, may choose to take control of the household and consider itself the top-ranking pack member.

Picking Up the Puppy

Teach family members that the proper way to pick up a puppy is to place one hand under its chest from the front while supporting its hindquarters with the other hand. The muscles and tendons of the fore-assembly can be torn or sprained by attempting to lift the puppy by pulling on the front legs.

Picking up the puppy the right way: one hand is under the chest, the other hand and arm supports the puppy's weight from the hind quarters.

The dog has to learn over and over that, although it is an integrated family member, the humans still outrank it. In short, you can allow your pet to do anything and everything, provided it stops immediately on your command.

The following are a few small exercises in submission:

1. The dog is allowed to lie on the sofa, but has to get down at once—without grumbling—when you direct it to do so.

2. It blocks access to a door, but stands up immediately to let you pass through when you so direct it.

3. You offer a dog treat, but the dog must first "sit" before receiving it.

4. The dog brings a ball, inviting you to throw it, but must *"Give it"* to you in your hand upon command from you, or *"Drop it"* in front of you, if that is the command given.

If your dog does not comply, you need to think about your own role in its lack of compliance. What is it that you have done to contribute to the dog's lack of compliance?

Children and Dogs

As a family dog, your pet also has to subordinate itself to children or at least to tolerate them. However, the way you raise your children plays an important role in determining whether you and your pet live in harmony.

Smaller children: Smaller children should not be allowed to play with the puppy without supervision. With its sharp little baby teeth the puppy could give your child a painful nip. The permanent adult teeth, which are not as sharp as puppy teeth come in around five months of age. Because of the unpredictable activities of small children around dogs or other animals, it is not wise to leave a small child alone with an adult dog.

Older children: Older children have to learn to respect the dog and to treat it properly. Children should be taught that the dog is not a toy, but a living creature that people must care for and cherish. The child will need to learn what is appropriate behavior and what can cause harm. When the dog is in its resting-place, such as its crate, its retreat to that place should be respected as an indication that it does not want to be disturbed.

Have your dog on a leash in public parks.

Not Everyone Is a Dog Lover

As our population continues to grow and our community public space becomes more crowded, keeping a dog in the city will be possible in the future only if owners behave responsibly with their dogs in public. Not everyone wants to have a dog greet him or her; it may bother or annoy other people, even if your dog is friendly. You should set a good example with your German Shepherd Dog by training it properly, thereby making a good impression in public and creating good will for our breed.

Public areas and parks: In public areas and parks, always keep the dog on a leash. It is not acceptable to let your pet play and romp hundreds of yards away from you. Someone who

is approaching you and who is afraid of dogs needs to see clearly that you have your pet under control. Also, there is no way you can know how other dogs will behave toward your pet.

Droppings: Never leave your pet's droppings for others to pick up. Be prepared at all times to pick up any droppings your dog may leave. This applies to grassy expanses in parks, motels, or public boulevards as well. The only area that you can postpone picking up droppings is in your own private yard. Every other time you are responsible for picking them up promptly. You can buy scoops and recyclable bags in pet stores or supermarkets or recycle the plastic bags of your own for this purpose.

Start the following exercises when your dog is about six or seven months old (for puppy training and training rules, see pages 47–49; for information on collars and leashes, see pages 31–32).

The Down Exercise

Start with the dog, on leash, sitting at your left. With your right hand, slowly place a treat on the ground right in front of your pet's nose. When it lowers its nose to the ground as well, move the treat forward a little, giving the *down* command at the same time. The dog will lie down to get to the treat. Give your pet its reward as soon as both the front of its body and its hindquarters are flat on the ground.

Pet your dog to keep it in this position for a few seconds. Next, direct it to sit again, then to stand. Keep practicing—never more than three times in a row, however—until the dog lies down in response to the *down* command alone. Gradually extend the time it maintains that position to one minute.

Down and Stay

When the dog can be counted on to perform the *down* command, from beside the dog hold the left hand, palm toward the dog and arm outstretched. Then slowly take one or two steps away, while giving the *stay* command. As you do so, praise the dog in a soft voice and tell it to stay lying down.

Important: If the dog wants to come to you, quickly say *"No"* and take a step toward the dog. If that doesn't help, repeat *"No"* with indignation, return the dog to the *down* position, and start the exercise over again.

Start with a few seconds, and gradually extend the dog's waiting time (up to two minutes) and your distance from the dog. Do not give the *release* signal until you have gone back to your dog, which should be still in the *down* position. Repeat this exercise a few times. Remember that you should never call your dog to come to you from its *down* position or you will not be able to rely on it to maintain that *down* position in the future.

The Stand Exercise

Have your pet sit—on leash—at your left side. Hold the leash and a treat in your right hand. As you move the treat out in front of you, away from the dog's nose, the leash will grow taut. Encourage your pet to get to its feet by simultaneously saying *"Stand."*

"Down" can be taught soon after the dog reliably "sits" on command. With your dog sitting, direct its attention to a treat and move the treat to ground level. As the dog drops his head to the treat, move it forward. The dog will lie down in order to get the treat.

Once the dog is on its feet, keep it in this position for several seconds by gently placing your left hand on the inside of its left thigh and giving it its treat, while saying a few soothing words. Then release it again with the *release* command. Soon it will move from the *sit* position to the *stand* position on the *stand* command alone.

Stand and stay: Once the dog has mastered the *stand* exercise, you can teach it the *stand and stay* exercise.

The Heel Exercise

By now the puppy has learned not to tug at the leash. At the age of six to seven months it is ready to practice walking with the leash slack, keeping its right shoulder even with your left foot, in response to the *heel* command.

Collar and leash: Use a link collar, set so as not to pull, and a leash sturdy enough to be jerked without breaking.

How to proceed: Start with the dog sitting at your left side. Holding the leash in your right hand, shorten it so that it hangs barely slack. Say *"Heel"* and walk forward, starting off with your left foot.

If the dog lags behind, encourage it to come along. If it forges ahead, correct it with a short, vigorous jerk on the leash with your left hand, at lightning speed (see Leash Training, page 48). At the same time, stand still, then move forward only a step at a time, once the dog is back in the right place.

Important: After the jerk, you should immediately let the leash hang slack again. If you maintain the tension or even pull the dog back, it will intensify its efforts to move forward.

Incorporating changes in pace: At first, don't walk too fast. Increase your tempo only when the dog is moving correctly. If it slows down, don't drag it along behind you; instead,

With the leash slack, the dog heels, keeping its shoulder even with your left leg.

use body language, verbal encouragement, and a faster pace to encourage it to catch up. Always go from your normal tempo to a faster or slower pace.

Practicing changes of direction: To keep your dog alert, don't walk in a straight line all the time. If the dog tries to change course, make a sudden about-face turn to the right or a precise right turn with a short jerk on the leash. Make a left turn if the dog is starting to go ahead of you. At the same time, use body language; for example, bend your knees slightly when making the turns.

Heeling Off Leash

Do not try heeling without the leash until your dog can execute certain exercises—straight ahead, right turn, left turn, about-face turn, normal pace, slow pace, and *run*—with the leash slack and while staying close to your left leg, without needing any leash corrections.

Important: Never let the dog run loose near a heavily traveled street. Being an animal, it will react instinctively and unpredictably, despite the best training. If accidents occur, you are responsible.

ACTIVITIES AND ADVANCED TRAINING

The German Shepherd Dog, with its multitude of talents and abilities, must have meaningful, appropriate activities and training. The most common cause of behavior problems is that the training the dog has received is inappropriate and inconsistent and the dog's desire for an activity is unfulfilled.

Play and Fitness

With its intelligence and desire to work, this dog enjoys learning as it plays and carries out tasks. Playing together not only will keep your pet physically and mentally fit, but also will contribute substantially to a good relationship between you and your dog. Today, you have many opportunities for engaging in recreational sports with your dog. In addition, you can join a good dog-training club in your area (see Information, page 92).

Important: Discuss with your veterinarian the activities in which you wish to engage your dog. Your veterinarian can advise you if these activities will be suitable for your dog or if

Agility is an organized competitive sport that is fun for the dog and the owner.

your dog has any health condition that will prevent it from being able to participate.

Finding a Good Dog Club

Do not choose a club until you have visited its training center and have had an opportunity to observe the classes and methods of training being used. The following questions will help you assess the club:

✔ Does the club offer puppy socialization and multiple levels of training classes?

✔ Are you and your pet given a friendly reception?

✔ Is your dog being evaluated primarily in terms of its suitability for training?

✔ Do the members treat their own dogs with kindness?

An advanced trained utility dog finding a "scented" article with his nose.

✔ Do the classes cover theory as well as practice?
✔ Are force-training methods or inducement-training methods used during the training sessions?

All-Breed Training Clubs

Most metropolitan areas have a number of AKC-affiliated training clubs from which to choose. Those training clubs welcome all breeds of dogs, including toy breeds, hounds, terriers, sporting dogs, non-sporting dogs, working dogs, and herding dogs. They offer basic obedience training for the average pet owner but will also offer advanced training that prepares those who seek to compete with their dogs in AKC competition events such as obedience, agility, rally, and tracking to name a few.

Specialty Breed Clubs

There are specialty clubs that are devoted to the purpose of providing German Shepherd Dog enthusiasts an opportunity to train their dogs in an environment where the other dogs present are also German Shepherd Dogs. Some of these clubs will offer multiple levels of training as well.

Working Dog Clubs

There are also specialty clubs that are devoted primarily to the German Shepherd Dog and specifically to promoting the working ability of the German Shepherd Dog. The German Shepherd Dog Club of America—Working Dog Association is the national club that has member regional clubs across the United States that offer training of dogs in a formalized and advanced sport operating under international rules. In working dog clubs and elsewhere in the world, this sport is known as Schutzhund and incorporates tests for obedience, tracking, temperament, and working abilities of the dog. The AKC has approved the Working Dog Sport for the German Shepherd Dog Club of America, the Doberman Pinscher

Club of America, the American Bouvier des Flandres Club, and the American Rottweiler Club. The event may be held only for these breeds at their National Specialties effective January 1, 2007. As the interest in this sport grows it is anticipated that other breeds whose history includes international participation in Schutzhund will seek AKC approval for this event as well.

The Right Trainer

Appropriate programs of basic and advanced training for dogs stand or fall with the quality of the club's trainers. Since no formal qualifications are required for this honorary function, you need to judge for yourself, using the following criteria.

A good trainer will

1. Present the club to you in its entirety, as well as tell you about the various training objectives and facilities for sports.

2. Gather information about your dog's special characteristics or problems as well as your purpose in training your pet.

3. Not only teach you the mechanical procedures, but also explain to you why his or her way of handling the dog's practical training is appropriate.

Sports Take Time

At least during the training phase, you will need to devote time to your dog. This will impact on the time you have for other leisure activities. With that in mind, the following is suggested:

1. Take your dog to the club early on the day of training for warm-up exercises.

2. Provide two to four 10-minute to 30-minute training sessions a day to practice what you have learned from the club trainer.

3. Keep in mind that trials or competitions are often held on weekends.

Exercise with Your Dog

Walking

Ten to thirty minutes of outdoor playtime or a walk, three to four times a day, is a reasonable approximation of the time that you should expect to spend keeping your dog healthy and physically fit. You should provide contact with the outside world for your dog in the form of walks in the neighborhood, local parks, and dog training centers. The dog needs to get to know the neighbors, its environment, and meet other members of its species. Limiting the outdoor

Retrieving a wooden dumbbell over a high jump is an exercise in "Open" obedience competition.

This dog uses its nose to find a hidden object. This "go find" game can be incorporated into your walks.

time only to your own backyard does not provide sufficient socialization.

Bicycling

Do not take the dog with you as a companion on a bike ride until its physical development is complete (about 18 months of age). The dog—on leash—should run at the right side of the bike, on the side away from any possible car or foot traffic. Start with ten minutes of biking and gradually increase that time as the dog learns to run with the bike and increases its endurance. Long trips of more than one hour could harm the dog, because it cannot control

the pace or limit the exercise according to its own capacity. If the dog obeys all your commands and if it has learned to run correctly beside the bicycle, this is a good exercise for dog and owner. Parks are a good place to start this routine as the dog can run on the grass while you are on the pavement. Running short stretches on pavement will toughen the pads; gradually increase the time on the pavement so the pads do not become injured.

Tracking

Tracking, in the form of a game, can be integrated into your walk. Having a second person, someone known to the dog, to accompany you would be helpful and provide some variation in the games you can play. While your pet stays behind with your companion, you walk away and hide behind a tree. You can mark your path every few yards with treats. When your companion gives the *"Go find"* command, the dog will begin to track you. When it finds you, shower it with praise. Or, bring an object that has your scent, such as a glove and drop it without attracting the dog's attention to it, at a designated place that you will remember during your walk. A few yards away turn back and give the *"Go find"* command. When he comes upon the object (with your help if necessary) drop treats on the object and reward him with praise.

The dog needs to be able to set the pace, and it has to be well-trained and healthy before undertaking exercise with a person on a bicycle.

Courage and physical agility are required for negotiating this dog walk. Teach your dog slowly on leash. Treats can also be used for motivation.

Agility

Agility provides fitness training for both dog and owner.

Obstacle course: An obstacle course, which varies in design from event to event, has to be negotiated by the dog and directed by its handler, without errors and as speedily as possible. In contrast to obedience, where the handler is always at the dog's side, here the dog is supposed to be controlled from certain distances as well.

Activities with Your Dog

Canine Good Citizen

The Canine Good Citizen is an AKC title that your dog can obtain after the completion of a basic program in socialization and obedience. Training centers usually provide a series of classes to prepare you and your dog and complete the series by offering the test that demonstrates the successful acceptance of a stranger including sitting for petting and allowing a stranger to brush or comb your dog. You and your dog will be asked to demonstrate walking on a leash, walking through a "crowd," and following the *sit, down, stay,* and *come* commands. Your dog's reaction to another dog will be observed as well

as its reaction to a sudden loud or distracting noise. The final observation will be that of your dog's tolerance to being left with someone else while you go out of sight for three minutes.

Obedience

Most German Shepherd Dogs will enjoy training and participation in obedience exercises. Many of them have a strong work ethic and

With a treat as an incentive, speed and agility are quickly learned through these weave poles in the agility course.

Teaching the puppy to accept petting from a stranger is required in the AKC Canine Good Citizen test, and it will prepare the puppy for obedience training.

an eagerness to learn new tasks. These dogs will look eagerly to their owners for something to do and seem to ask, "What can I do to please you?" The participation in obedience training classes provides the opportunity for you to learn how to command your dog's respect and provide it with challenging activities that it will look forward to each week.

The AKC Obedience Competition provides three levels of obedience: Novice, Open, and Utility.

• At the Novice level the exercises are the basic heeling on and off leash, standing for examination, coming when called, and the *sit* and *down/stay* exercises.

• Open exercises are obedience exercises done off leash and include jumping and retrieving exercises.

• Utility exercises use hand signals for the obedience exercises. Incorporated into this level of obedience is an exercise in scent discrimination

and directed retrieving as well as directed jump exercises.

Rally

Rally is a new addition to the AKC competition exercises offered for titles. In Rally, the dog needs to know a large number of obedience and jumping exercises and must perform them at its handler's direction. The course is not the same at each trial and the handler must be adaptable and quickly think on his or her feet as they determine the exercise in the proper order that is required of them and their dog.

Flyball

In this sport, two teams, each with four dogs, start at the same time. Each dog, at its handler's command, has to clear four relatively small hurdles, press down the pedal of a ball machine, catch the ball tossed out by the machine, and carry it back over the four hurdles and across the finish line. If it has crossed the line without making a mistake, the next dog in the group can start the course. The team that is the first to have all four dogs cross the finish line without any mistake is the winner.

Working Dog Sport

The Working Dog Sport is still in development in the AKC and has been approved as an event at the German Shepherd Dog, the Bouvier des Flandres, the Rottweiler, and the Doberman Pinscher National Specialty Shows. The sport is also known as the sport of Schutzhund, organized under international rules. Many clubs in many parts of the world engage in this sport. Schutzhund originated to provide a test to evaluate the character and working ability of breeding animals. It is used to test the temperament of the German Shepherd Dog and other working breeds. It also provides the German Shepherd Dog with an activity that satisfies its need to have an active and useful "job."

Schutzhund

Schutzhund I is the first level of achievement in this sport. The intermediate level is Schutzhund II and the highest and most demanding achievement is Schutzhund III. Each level demands additional compliance with the expectations of obedience, including heeling, recall, and retrieval. There are components of tracking and courage or protection in each level that present new challenges. Only those dogs that are of sound temperament, sound physical structure, and reliably follow commands will succeed in the completion of these titles of achievement.

Obedience: The obedience component of the working dog sport tests the dog's ability and willingness to work under the direction of its handler. It combines heeling and other standard obedience requirements with agility and retrieving objects.

Tracking: Tracking tests the dog's instinctive ability to use its nose to find the trail of a person over changing terrain and varying distances. The dog must also find objects dropped by the person along the trail and must follow the track precisely.

Protection: This component of the Working Dog Sport tests the courage of the dog and the trainer's ability to direct this courage and mold the character in developing a well-behaved and responsible dog. The dog has to find a hidden "suspect," alert the handler to the suspect's location, and cause no harm to the suspect being held at bay. The dog has to resist an attack upon itself or its handler, catch the fleeing suspect, and respond without hesitation. The dog must release the suspect immediately upon command and must be on alert and guard should the suspect again attempt to flee. To pass this part of the event, the dog must show good temperament, a courageous heart, and strict obedience to its handler.

Participation in a club that promotes the Working Dog Sport can help you achieve personal goals by providing recreation with your dog, a better understanding of dog training, and the opportunity to develop your dog into a sound, well-rounded companion. You may find that you enjoy the precise training that leads to participation and competition in the formalized sport.

Holding a suspect at bay.

FEEDING AND NUTRITION

Like its ancient ancestor, the wolf, the dog is also a meat-eating or carnivorous animal. In the strict sense, however the term "meat eater" is not entirely accurate, since the wolf does not eat the flesh of its prey exclusively.

The First Days at Home

In general, the recommendations of the breeder from whom you have obtained your puppy should be followed precisely for the first two weeks. The puppy is making many adjustments in its routine and it does not need the additional stress of having its food changed—a change in the food or the feeding times can be most disruptive. If the puppy stops eating or develops diarrhea and you have changed its diet, then you and the breeder will have more difficulty figuring out the problem. Stress can cause a puppy to stop eating and a change in water alone can cause a puppy to develop diarrhea until it adjusts to the water; you don't need one more variation in making the adjustment. Any food changes must be made gradually over a ten-day period.

It is critical to meet the nutritional needs of your German Shepherd Dog from puppyhood through maturity.

As Your Puppy Grows

Follow your breeder's recommendations or use the following guidelines:
• At nine weeks of age feed three-fourths of a cup three times a day.
• At twelve weeks of age feed one and one-fourth cup three times a day.
• At sixteen weeks of age make a transition to two level cups two times a day.
• At six months of age you should be feeding approximately two and one-half cups twice a day.
• Beyond six months the food should be adjusted for the size and activity of the dog but even adult German Shepherd Dogs should be fed twice a day for the balance of their lifetime. Two smaller meals are healthier for your dog than one large meal.

Water

In all cases put water over the food. This is healthy and convenient because it allows the

Plan ahead to enable yourself to provide access to fresh water to your dog when needed on outings.

be easily felt through the skin. You would want to see only the last two to three ribs when looking at the puppy. The puppy should have a "waistline" at the age of three to four months and older.

The stool or droppings should have a moist appearance and be formed. A stool that appears dry and breaks up indicates that the puppy is not getting enough to eat. A stool that is wet and unformed is an indication that the puppy is overfed. You will learn to distinguish between the unformed stool of a healthy overfed puppy and that of a sick puppy. A stool with mucus in it or a ring of liquid around it is suspicious for illness.

puppy to take in water with the food that would otherwise require the puppy to consume more water on the side. Fresh water should be available at all times in addition to that offered in the food.

Monitor Weight

You will need to monitor the weight of your puppy and adjust the amount of feeding, increasing it by no more than ten percent at a time as the puppy grows. The increases are fairly frequent until the puppy is about six months of age at which time the amount levels out or decreases slightly, depending upon the activity level of the puppy. Monitor the weight of the puppy by feeling the rib cage and by observing the consistency of the stool or bowel movement droppings. The ribs should

Ending Puppy Food

Continue feeding a puppy formula as the breeder recommends, until the puppy attains adult full height at six to eight months, or until 12 to 15 months of age for very active dogs. When making the change from puppy food to adult formula, plan ahead to make this change gradually over a ten-day period. Without changing the total quantity of food being fed, add ten percent of the adult formula and remove ten percent of the puppy food each day as long as the stools remain formed. If at any time the stools are not normal, go back to the ratio of puppy food to adult formula from the day before and do not make any further changes until the stools are again normal. Then begin the progression again, changing only ten percent a day until a full adult feeding is achieved.

TIP

Panosteitis

In addition to breeder's recommendation, there is one other time when puppies that are five to eight months of age might be placed on adult formula. This is if they develop *panosteitis*, which is a condition seen in German Shepherd Dogs during a rapid growth phase. Panosteitis is an inflammation of the long bones and can be diagnosed by veterinarians by X-ray or palpation. Experienced breeders are able to make this determination and assist with the management of it as well. Many recommend that panosteitis be treated aggressively to avoid having compensatory structural changes or to avoid having the condition become chronic.

A puppy grows rapidly between four and eight months of age.

Choosing a Diet

Most conscientious breeders will guide your selection of an appropriate commercial food, in which case you would be wise to follow those recommendations. Discuss this with the breeder before it is time to take your puppy home so that you can be prepared. Some breeders will even include a specific brand of food as a part of the written contract.

Changes in Diet

Good commercial foods from well-known dog food manufacturers are recommended. These dog food manufacturers have conducted extensive testing for formulas that will produce successful results. A German Shepherd Dog will reach skeletal maturity between fifteen months and two years of age. During this long growth period the puppy needs controlled calories with moderate fat content for proper skeletal growth without excessive weight gain. German Shepherd Dogs also have a sensitive digestive system and do not tolerate changes in their food. It is important to make the selection of the diet carefully so that, other than from puppy food to adult formula, changes do not need to be made during the lifetime of the dog. Dogs do not need variety in their daily food consumption. They look forward to their regular food at regular times and do not tolerate change very well.

"Raw Diets"

There are some that recommend feeding a "raw diet" or preparing your dog's food yourself

No Bones about It

Bones are not a suitable food for dogs. There is a danger of constipation and an even greater danger of splinters resulting in intestinal perforation or obstruction. Supervised gnawing on prepared large beef bones can be useful in combating tartar on the teeth but poultry, venison, or pork bones will splinter and cause serious damage to the intestines and can precipitate a medical emergency. Better are the synthetic chew bones or Nylabones that are readily available at pet stores. Nylabones provide the benefit of tartar removal and provide a bored adult with a toy. Gummybones give a teething puppy a safe and suitable alternative to bones.

from meat, vegetables, and cereals. I cannot recommend this—it is expensive and difficult. It also requires that you be extremely precise in combining foods and adding the appropriate nutrients in just the right amounts for a healthy well-balanced diet. It is time-consuming and demands total dedication to studying the nutritional requirements of the dog and providing for changes in activity levels. Raw meats, poultry, and fish may contain bacteria that can be transmitted to your pet and the illness that results can be fatal in dogs.

Commercial Dog Food

Most well-known brand-name commercial dog foods are precisely formulated to meet the dog's nutritional needs. There are specific nutritional requirements at various ages and within brands there are specific diets that are formulated for stages from puppyhood to adult to senior care. There are also brands that formulate diets for the needs of the German Shepherd Dog as a specific breed or as one of the breeds in the class of large-breed dogs. These formulas take into account the average growth rate of a German Shepherd Dog from birth to an adult weight of 60 to 90 pounds (27–41 kg). These premium brands offer several formulas that contain all the substances that are important in a healthy diet for a dog. The formulas for puppies and adults offered for large breeds are suitable for the German Shepherd Dog. Supplements are neither advised nor required when using a good brand of dog food.

Where and When to Feed

Where: The food and water utensils should always be placed in the same spot. The dog will come to expect to be fed in that location.

When: Give young dogs three meals a day; even an adult dog needs to be fed twice a day. It is better for its health and is less stressful for the dog's digestive system.

✔ Feed your pet at the same times of day. There can be occasional exceptions to that but if you have caused your dog to miss a meal, do not attempt to make up for it by feeding twice the amount at one feeding. To do that is to risk digestive upset, toxic gut or gastric torsion, and bloat in your pet. If your dog misses an occasional meal, it is far healthier to eat the regular amount at the next scheduled feeding time.

It won't be long before this puppy is as big as its mother.

✔ Don't feed your German Shepherd Dog immediately after strenuous activity. Following a meal, active play, jogging, or other work should be postponed for two to three hours to decrease the chances of gastric torsion and bloat (see pages 88–89).

Water

Fresh water has to be available to your pet at all times. When traveling with your German Shepherd Dog you will want to bring along water from home in a clean container in sufficient quantities to last for the time that you are gone. German Shepherd Dogs do not tolerate changes in water from area to area. Many dogs will develop diarrhea with water change. An alternative is to purchase bottled drinking water (not distilled water) for your dog. Bottled water is readily available everywhere and if you plan to bring water for your own drinking, it is easy enough to allow for the quantity your dog will drink as well. Be aware that milk can cause diarrhea and is not a substitute for water.

Overweight Dogs

Excess weight poses many health risk factors for a dog and can substantially shorten its life and decreases the quality of life for those that are overweight. Shortness of breath, heart and circulatory problems, digestive problems and excessive stress on tendons and joints are only a few examples.

The "figure" test: If you can no longer easily feel the dog's ribs at mid-chest level behind its shoulder blades, and your dog no longer has a discernible "waistline," then it is too fat. Careful reduction of the excess weight is called for.

Healthy weight loss: First and foremost, have a veterinarian confirm that the dog is overweight due to simple excess food consumption. The veterinarian may detect possible disease conditions that are causes for the extra pounds. Depending on the causes of the excess weight, the veterinarian will prescribe a weight-loss diet for the dog. There are excellent diet foods commercially available either from your veterinarian or in pet stores to help you control your dog's weight.

Avoid the Problem

It is best to avoid the overweight condition by regularly monitoring the weight your dog is carrying. Look at your dog's physical structure critically.

GROOMING AND HEALTH

Regular grooming of a dog is an important hygienic measure, a necessary procedure whenever humans and animals live together. Bathing your pet to get it clean is necessary only every six months with daily brushing.

Start Grooming Early

Well-groomed dogs are less disease-prone, and giving your animal attention in this way strengthens the bond between you and your dog.

It is best to get your pet used to grooming procedures, such as taking care of its coat, inspecting its teeth, and cleaning its ears, while it is still a puppy, even though these procedures are performed on a much smaller scale than in the case of a full-grown dog.

By starting early, your pet will learn what it is like to be lifted onto a table, to keep quiet, to stand still, and to lie down, and as an adult dog it will be more apt to enjoy the grooming process than to submit to it reluctantly.

Daily coat care keeps your German Shepherd Dog healthy as well as beautiful. Spending time with your pet while grooming it deepens the bond between you and your dog.

Health Check from A to Z

During grooming, which involves close contact with the dog, you also need to be on the lookout for any symptoms of disease. Changes in behavior are the first noticeable signs of a possible illness. The animal will appear sad, listless, surly, or ill-tempered. It moves around from one place to another, is restless, runs aimlessly to and fro, whimpers, groans, cries out when touched, howls, or is fearful or confused. It seems indifferent to its surroundings, has a vacant stare, moves slowly and haltingly, or sleeps a great deal.

During the grooming process you may notice physical symptoms of illness as well. Pay attention to the following:

Bad breath: Diseased teeth or a stomach ailment may be the cause. Consult the veterinarian.

Body build: Substantial weight loss or gain may be a symptom of disease.

Body temperature: The normal temperature of a dog is between 100 and 102.5°F (37.5–38°C (see Taking the Dog's Temperature, page 84).

Coat: Dull, dry hair with a reddish tinge, as well as brittle hair, often are signs of malnutrition. However, it is normal for the coat to lose its gloss before new hair growth occurs in spring and fall.

Ears: If the dog repeatedly tilts its head to one side, shakes it frequently, and keeps scratching at its ear, it probably has dirt in its inner ear or an ear infection due to ear mites. Their presence can cause a dark, dirty, waxy material to adhere to the inner skin of the ears. If you suspect ear mites, seek professional help to combat these pests, which are usually transmitted through contract with infected animals.

Eyes: They should be clear. Reddened eyes and a discharge are indications of conjunctivitis; clouded eyes point to some other disease. See a veterinarian.

Feet: Nails have to be clipped (see page 75). When grooming this area, also check for injuries

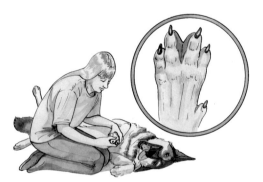

Check the areas between the toes and under the toe pads for injury or foreign objects, such as weed stickers and burrs. Toenails need to be trimmed regularly.

on your pet's feet and foreign bodies between its toes.

Gums and mucous membranes of the mouth: The gums and mucous membranes of the mouth should be rose pink in color. Some very dark German Shepherd Dogs will have a lot of black coloration in the gums. You should be able to find some areas that do not have dark pigment so that you can observe the typical pink color of the gums. Reddened gums are a sign of inflammation that may be from diseased teeth or tartar accumulation. Pale gums or mucous membranes may be a sign of serious illness or impending shock. Make a habit of looking at the color of the gums and touching them lightly with your fingertip to see the response of the gums when the dog is its normal active self. The gums will blanche with a light touch and the color bounces right back when you take your finger off.

Lips, flews: (Flews are pendulous upper lips overhanging the lower jaw or loose lower lips that droop.) Lips in a German Shepherd Dog should be firmly fitted. There are some German Shepherd Dogs whose flews naturally droop slightly. When that is the case, the lips, not infrequently, are affected by chapping or lip eczema, where hard crusts form at the corners of the mouth. The lips may lose pigment and crust over which may be a sign of infection. You will want to have your dog seen by a veterinarian for treatment. The crusting and infection may be caused by the use of rawhide chew toys or other chew toys that are causing a lip abrasion. If rawhide chew toys have caused this in your dog, it is likely to cause it again and again, in which case it would be best to substitute another type of chew toy, as some dogs just do not tolerate chewing on rawhide. In the case of the nylon chew toys that may have caused this, it is a sign that the chew toy has been around too long and it is time to get a new one.

Pulse rate: The dog's heart beats 60 to 80 times a minute. The rate can rise because of anxiety, fear, or happiness, and after physical exertion. Take your pet's pulse on the inside of its thigh where there is a large artery that is easy to feel. Practice doing this, on occasion, until you are comfortable that you can palpate the pulse. At rest, the dog takes 12 to 20 breaths a minute.

Skin: When a dog receives proper nutrition and is groomed regularly, it is less likely to suffer from common skin problems. Symptoms of disease include discoloration of the skin on the inner thighs and abdomen, dry scaling patches, greasy-smelling dandruff or seborrhea, foul-smelling exudate (moist eczema or "hot spots"), frequent itching and scratching, and loss of hair. Some dogs are subject to sebaceous cysts, which are small round lumps in the skin that can exude a whitish material that then crusts over. These can become infected as well. Most problematic skin conditions require treatment from a veterinarian and will respond more readily to treatment if attended to soon after the problem is noticed.

Stool: The dog's stool should be firm, compact, not overly hard, and sausage-shaped. See your veterinarian if there is diarrhea accompanied by blood in the stool, diarrhea accompanied by either vomiting or fever, or diarrhea that goes on longer than a day. When you notice diarrhea, withhold food for a day, offer plenty of water, and closely monitor the dog for any other sign of not feeling well. If the dog seems fine and its activity level is normal, the diarrhea may resolve itself. If the dog does not have a normal activity level, appears to be ill, or

Lift the lips to check the color and health of the gums and teeth. Check the lips for injury or crusting.

if the gums are pale or the color does not bounce back when the gums are pressed lightly and released, consult a veterinarian immediately.

Teeth: Plaque, tartar, or dental calculus is a yellowish deposit on the teeth and can be prevented by daily brushing of the teeth or by providing chew toys that are designed to help remove tartar and plaque. Some dogs enjoy the attention they are getting during the brushing routine. Do not use toothpaste made for humans, it is not intended to be consumed and dogs will swallow it. There is doggy toothpaste available at pet stores as well as "dental" toys. Some dog owners are willing to purchase and learn how to use dental scrapers to remove tartar. Ask your veterinarian about this is you wish to do this yourself at home.

Urine: The dog's urine should be released in a stream, not in drops. It should be a pale yellow

Important: If at any time you think your pet may be ill, even though you cannot tell why, see the veterinarian without delay!

to darker yellow in color. Blood in the urine is abnormal. It may indicate a kidney stone, a bladder stone, or a urinary tract infection. A dog that has blood-tinged urine should be seen immediately by a veterinarian.

Should I Bathe My Dog?

The short hair of the German Shepherd Dog is very easy to take care of, and it does not get dirty easily; a daily brushing, however, is advisable. The double coat consists of the so-called top, or outer, coat and the undercoat. The hairs of the former lie like roof shingles on the dog's skin and protect the undercoat against dampness.

As a rule, German Shepherd Dogs enjoy the water. When the weather is hot, they love to play with the water hose and to take a little shower in the yard. Therefore, bathing your pet to get it clean—unless it is extremely dirty or smelly—is necessary only during spring and fall, when its new coat is growing in.

Summer: In summer, after you bathe your pet and have towel-dried it thoroughly, go for a walk with the dog on leash, to give the coat

How to Bathe Your Dog

✔ Place the dog on a nonskid surface in the bathtub.

✔ Using a moisturizing shampoo for dogs, put some in a small container and dilute it with lukewarm water.

✔ Spray the dog thoroughly with lukewarm water, then rub the shampoo into its coat, keeping one hand over its eyes to shield them.

✔ Rinse the dog thoroughly again. If necessary, repeat the process.

✔ Finally, towel-dry the dog well.

an opportunity to dry completely. It is important to dry the coat thoroughly, especially the thick fur under the neck, behind the shoulders, and the folds between the legs and body. In the warm weather and especially in damp conditions, bacteria loves to grow—not drying the dog completely will set up conditions for "hot spots" and other skin problems.

Winter: In winter, be sure to towel-dry the coat thoroughly; take your dog for a quick outside walk to give the dog the opportunity to shake the excess moisture off the coat. The balance of the drying time should be done indoors. Activities that keep the dog moving around the house will assist the drying process.

Dryers: Human hair dryers should not be used as they can damage the skin and are too drying for the dog's skin and hair. There are dog blow dryers available at pet stores that do not use heat but only forced air to blow the excess water out of the hair. The coat is typically still damp following this blow drying process.

Note: There are pet stores or shops that provide "do it yourself" bathing facilities and grooming tools for owners to use at a modest cost. If you do not have a convenient arrangement at home for bathing your dog, you may wish to look into those options.

Combing and Brushing

To keep your German Shepherd Dog's coat glossy, you need to comb and brush it daily.

How to do it:

✔ Position the dog with the front of its body slightly elevated, so that its skin will be taut (for example, put its front paws on the lowest stair of your staircase).

✔ With a hard-bristled brush, brush the hair with long strokes, against the lie.

Many dogs love to go swimming but their skin and hair should be rinsed of saltwater and algae and dried thoroughly to prevent skin problems.

✔ Next, brush the hair smooth again, with the lie.

✔ Finally, use a comb to remove loose hairs. Comb the tail thoroughly with a wide-toothed comb.

Note: During shedding season, use a special shedding comb and a comb to remove loose undercoat hairs.

Elbow Care

Over time, leathery, sometimes cracked areas develop on the elbows that then may turn into toughened hairless callouses. This happens because the dog supports its weight on its elbows when it lies down. Sometimes, swelling occurs over the elbows, if this swelling persists, if the callouses are wet or weep, or if the dog is lame, consult your veterinarian.

Anal Care

If the anal sacs do not empty themselves when the dog has a bowel movement, they may get "full." This may cause the dog some discomfort and it may "scoot" around on its bottom. Take your dog to the veterinarian, who will be able to empty the sacs. Have the veterinarian show you where these anal sacs are located. If this becomes a frequent problem for your dog, the veterinarian may also show you how to empty the sacs at home, if you are inclined to learn.

Perianal fistulas: German Shepherd Dogs are more likely than other breeds to get perianal fistulas. It is not the same as the anal sacs getting "full" but the attention that the animal gives the anal area by "scooting" and licking is similar. This is a chronic condition that will require veterinary treatment.

Note: Worms may also cause a dog to "scoot" around on its bottom. Take a stool sample to the veterinarian to test for worms.

TIP

Garlic

Add half a teaspoon of garlic to your pet's daily rations. Generally, it will act as a tick preventive.

Regular grooming is important not only to keep your dog looking good, but to keep it healthy as well. Essential procedures involved in grooming a dog are described below.

Grooming Utensils

You need appropriate "tools" for grooming. These include a shedding comb, a wide-toothed comb, a narrower toothed comb, a brush, a slicker brush, a toothbrush, nail clippers, a nail file, and tick tweezers.

Eye Care

You should check your dog's eyes on a daily basis. After it wakes up, use a damp tissue to remove any secretions that have accumulated in the corners of its eyes. You can soften encrusted matter with water (*not* boric acid solution) in advance. Check to see whether the conjunctiva is reddened or inflamed (see page 70).

Ear Care

If your pet's ears are dirty, put a few drops of ear cleanser (available from your veterinarian) into each ear. Next, carefully knead the outside of the ear at its base. After the dog shakes itself, clean the external part of the ear with a piece of cotton wrapped around your little finger. Do *not* use a cotton swab; it is all too easy to push it too deeply into the auditory canal and injure the eardrum.

Note: If the dog cries out in pain when you knead its ear from the outside, an inflammation is present. It is essential to take the dog to the veterinarian at once.

Dental Care

The teeth of your German Shepherd Dog have to be checked regularly. Some dogs have a tendency to tartar buildup, which can result in gingivitis and even in tooth loss. Tartar is visible as a brownish coating at the base of the tooth.

Regularly brushing your pet's teeth with a hard-bristled toothbrush (special toothpaste is available from the veterinarian or in a pet store; do *not* use toothpaste meant for humans) can prevent tartar. As an alternative, give the dog rawhide, Nylabones, or similar things to chew.

From time to time, rub the dog's teeth with a slice of lemon.

Note: If you do not keep up with the removal of plaque with a toothbrush or chew toy, it will harden and form tartar. Some pet owners are comfortable purchasing "tooth scrapers" and learning how to use them to remove the hardened tartar. This requires patience and steady

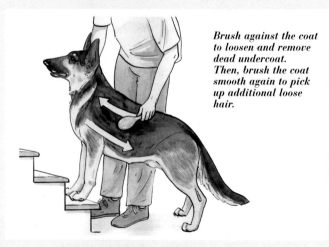

Brush against the coat to loosen and remove dead undercoat. Then, brush the coat smooth again to pick up additional loose hair.

hands but can be done. If you are so inclined to do this, start while your dog is a young adult and the plaque is not so hard. Find someone to teach you, such as your veterinarian. Some experienced breeders do this and may be willing to teach you how.

If you are not inclined to do this, you will need to arrange with your veterinarian to have an anesthetic administered to your dog followed by the dental cleaning procedures. You will usually be able to pick up your dog the same day. If you discover that your pet has a loose or broken tooth, if the dog drools excessively, or if it has bad breath, consult your veterinarian. These are signs of possible infection.

If the ears are dirty, a few drops of rubbing alcohol or ear cleaning solution placed in the external ear and wiped with a cotton ball will remove the debris.

Foot Care

There are foot care products available at pet stores and from your veterinarian for dry or cracked pads. The use of these products if you walk your dog on pavement can be helpful in conditioning the pads and preventing cracked and painful pads.

After a walk, check your dog's feet and remove any asphalt, small stones, or other foreign objects adhering to them. Look for burrs or other seeds that may get caught in the hair between the toe pads.

In winter, use a foot care product to protect your dog's feet against thawing chemicals or salt. When you come home from walks, wash the dirt and chemicals or salt off the paws with warm water in a shallow plastic tub, then dry the feet well with a towel.

Nail Care

Normally, active and working dogs will wear down the nails when the dog moves over hard surfaces such as concrete sidewalks. Many of our dogs do not get exercise on hard surfaces that will wear down the nails and older dogs move around less. In these cases, the nails may grow too long and become a hindrance to ease of movement and uncomfortable for the dog and need to be trimmed.

Let the veterinarian, or the breeder of your dog, show you how to clip your dog's nails. The problem is that blood vessels and nerve endings extend into the nails, and they can be injured when you trim the nail. It is better to trim nails a little bit, and more frequently, than to trim a lot off and hurt the dog—it will only make it harder to accomplish the next time.

Sharp nails in a puppy can be smoothed and rounded with a nail file or nipped with a nail clipper and then filed. Be sure that this experience is not unpleasant by having a second person give special treats, such as cheese chunks or dog treats, and distract the puppy while the person clipping the nails is working carefully so the puppy does not experience pain. Treats can work for older dogs as well.

PREVENTIVE CARE AND DISEASES

Even with proper care, your German Shepherd Dog may become sick. Many German Shepherd Dogs are very pain tolerant so it is up to you to be observant. A change in behavior, such as restlessness, pacing, or anxiously seeking attention, can be a sign of gastrointestinal emergency.

Your Dog's Health

If you notice changes in your pet's eating pattern, elimination routine, attitude, activity level, and behavior, or simply suspect that something is wrong with your dog, don't postpone the trip to the veterinarian. The earlier a problem is detected and treated, the better the chances for a quick recovery. Owners that familiarize themselves with common health problems and their symptoms and are observant will be able to recognize quickly when something is amiss.

Vaccinations

There are effective immunizations against rabies, distemper, hepatitis, canine parvovirus,

Preventive health care is a must in keeping your dog healthy.

and leptospirosis. To ensure complete immunity, the dog must be vaccinated according to a certain schedule. Your puppy should have gotten its first vaccinations before it leaves the breeder. Be sure that you have this vaccination record when you take your puppy for its first visit to the veterinarian. He or she will recommend the vaccinations that your puppy needs and the intervals at which they should be administered. The recommendations may include vaccination for Lyme disease if exposure to that disease is a concern in your area.

Schedule and Frequency

There are changes being made by the veterinary community in the schedule and frequency of booster injections. At one time boosters were given annually, but there are changes in the recommendations and some drug companies and veterinarians have found that boosters

It is important to keep an ongoing record of visits to the veterinarian, including vaccinations, medication, and other medical or surgical treatment.

every two to three years is sufficient. Some recent data indicates that there is life-time immunity for some vaccinations administered when the dog is 1 year or older. Some veterinarians are testing the blood for immunity levels and they use that as a guide as to when booster injections are needed.

Bordatella: Bordatella vaccination for kennel cough can be given nasally or by injection. Because kennel cough is highly contagious and immunity may last only six months, be sure that your dog is up to date on this vaccination if you are going to be on vacation or out of town and plan to kennel your dog while you are away.

Heartworm Prevention

If you live in an area where there are mosquitoes, you must protect your German Shepherd Dog from heartworm disease. This is a preventable disease. Prevention is accomplished with heartworm preventive medication administered monthly in a chewable tablet. Mosquitoes carry heartworm larvae. When a mosquito bites your dog, the larvae are deposited into the bloodstream. The larvae migrate into the body of the dog, grow to maturity, and take up residence in the heart and lungs. Left untreated, heartworm disease is fatal. While heartworm disease can be treated, it requires hospitalization and subsequent confinement during recovery. Treatment is hard on the dog; heartworm prevention is simple and effective. In some areas, veterinarians may advise administering the preventive year-round. Where mosquitoes are seasonal it is likely that your veterinarian will draw a blood sample in the early spring to check for heartworms before starting your dog on the preventive medication.

Parasite Control

Fleas

In some areas fleas cause the most problems—fleas bite and suck blood from the dog. Many dogs become allergic to flea saliva and have intense itching. Flea collars on a German Shepherd Dog have limited effectiveness and constantly expose the dog to insecticide, which is toxic and can be inhaled, not only by the dog but also by everyone who comes close to the dog. There are now once-a-month tablets that will control the flea problem as it sterilizes the eggs laid by the fleas, but it does not kill the adult flea. Consider this product following a flea bath and environmental decontamination if you live in an area where fleas are a constant problem.

✔ Environmental control is an important aspect of flea control as eggs can survive for long periods of time.

✔ Tackle this problem with your veterinarian early to have the best success in ridding the environment and your dog of fleas.

✔ Be particular in reading labels and take care to use products that are safe for your dog.

✔ Do not combine products without instructions from your veterinarian.

Fleas are difficult to manage in some areas of the United States. If you have a frequent problem with fleas, you may want to check your dog often for intestinal worms, since fleas transmit the most common tapeworm in dogs.

Ticks

Unless you live in an area with extremely heavy tick infestation, you can manage ticks by searching for them on your dog's coat, paying particular attention to the head, neck, and ears, to the areas where the legs join the body, on the feet, and between the pads. Spray them with rubbing alcohol, which is toxic to both fleas and ticks, and will cause ticks to loosen their grip, at which time you can pick them off. Some prefer to use tweezers to remove ticks. Ticks are surprisingly easy to feel when running your fingers through the coat. Work with your veterinarian to find a program of control if you frequent areas with severe tick infestation. Tick collars are toxic and some dogs (and toddlers) will eat them. Medications for ticks carry warnings and often are not effective for the length of time noted on the label. Combining products can make your dog very sick.

Removing Parasites

Fleas and ticks are among the most common parasites that infest dogs.

Fleas: Fleas can be picked up anywhere by your pet. They are especially active during the warm months of the year. If your dog scratches itself frequently, it may have fleas. Examine its coat thoroughly—flea excrement is visible as tiny, dark dots on the skin. Fleas also can be transmitted to humans.

The veterinarian or a pet store can supply you with a special shampoo for bathing your dog, or with a special powder and an anti-flea spray. You need to disinfect the place where the dog sleeps and the floor at the same time, because these little pests also are present in the dog's surroundings. It is important to repeat the treatment after about one week, since new fleas can hatch from eggs that have not been killed, and reinfest your pet.

Note: Tick and flea collars have only limited suitability, because they give off insecticides with which the dog will be in close physical contact.

During the entire time that your pet is wearing this tick and flea collar it is exposed to the insecticides while the collar targets only the fleas and ticks that are close enough to the collar to be affected. The pros and cons of constant exposure to insecticides must be weighed carefully with regard to the German Shepherd Dog. Discuss this with your veterinarian.

Ticks: They are especially common in warm, damp months. Check your pet's skin for ticks every time you return from a walk in the woods, and every time your dog has been in bushes or underbrush.

It is best to remove ticks with ordinary tweezers or with special tick tweezers (available in pet stores).

Use the tweezers to grab the tick as close to the dog's skin as possible, pulling *very* slowly on the tick's head and mouth. Be certain to get all of the tick out of your dog's skin, and then put alcohol or another antiseptic on the bite.

Not only are ticks a nuisance, they also carry a life-threatening disease: *Borelliosis* or *Lyme disease.*

Lyme disease, first identified in Lyme, Connecticut, is spread primarily by the deer tick, a tiny bloodsucker credited with carrying an illness that can do your dog—and you—great physical harm! Borelliosis can affect your dog in several ways, but usually swelling and tenderness around the joints are present. If you find a tick on your dog, or suspect that the dog has been bitten by a deer tick, contact your veterinarian immediately.

If you have been bitten by a deer tick or see the telltale tick bite surrounded by a characteristic red ring, consult your physician or county health department. In both cases—yours and the dog's—timely diagnosis and treatment are essential!

Intestinal Parasites

A full-grown dog should have its stool checked for intestinal parasites as part of the annual health check. The examination of the stool under a microscope may reveal intestinal worms such as hookworms, roundworms, tapeworms, or whipworms, as well as giardia and coccidia, which are other intestinal parasites that infect the dog and can cause diarrhea. In some cases, intestinal parasites may be present but not detected in the stool. If the dog has an intestinal problem that your veterinarian is trying to diagnose, you may be asked to bring in several samples on successive days. Worming and treatment for other intestinal parasite infections should be carried out under the guidance of your veterinarian. Routine worming is not recommended without evidence of infestation.

Spaying and Neutering

Unless you have purchased your puppy specifically for breeding or for show, you should discuss spaying (females) or neutering (males) with the breeder and your veterinarian. The breeder may have sold the animal to you under a spay or neuter contract or may have asked

German Shepherd Dogs love to spend time with their owners outdoors. It is important to keep them free of parasites that they can pick up when outside.

you to check back with him or her as the puppy develops so that the breeder can evaluate your dog for the purposes of showing. Animals that have been spayed or neutered are not eligible to be shown for their championship at AKC dog shows; they are eligible to compete in performance events at AKC shows.

Your veterinarian will have recommendations for the timing of this procedure. It is known that females spayed prior to their first heat will have a reduced incidence of mammary tumors or breast cancer. Neutering of males is recommended following growth to full size or between a year and eighteen months of age. Once spayed or neutered, the animals are no longer affected by the sex hormones. Some think that aggression in males can be eliminated by neutering but experienced breeders know that aggression is best avoided by proper socialization, consistent training, and raising a puppy to know that the humans in the pack are "top dogs" and that the dog is not.

This dog's bright expression, clear eyes, white teeth, and clean ears give evidence of good health and good grooming.

Proper socialization and training establish the proper human/dog "pack order."

Detecting Signs of Illness

In the chapter "Grooming and Health" behavioral changes are described that are indicators of disease. If the following symptoms appear, take your pet to the veterinarian without delay:

1. The dog refuses to eat.

2. It stops drinking water or has gone a long time without urinating.

3. It has diarrhea longer than one day.

4. It does not have a daily bowel movement or attempts to have a bowel movement but can't.

5. It vomits, drinks water, and vomits again, or repeatedly attempts to vomit but produces only a frothy mucus.

6. It has difficulty breathing and pants even at rest.

7. It sways, staggers, loses its balance, goes down, or loses consciousness.

8. It suffers from severe itching and bites at its feet or skin and creates open sores.

9. Its pulse is too high or too low at rest or the rate of breathing is too fast.

10. The dog has trouble getting to its feet, or is limping and whines and cries out when climbing stairs or walking.

11. Blood is present in the urine or stool.

12. It has a fever.

13. It is unusually restless, anxiously seeks your attention, or has difficulty finding a comfortable place to rest.

14. It is unusually quiet, seems "not quite itself," or is listless or reluctant to get up.

Note: Depending on the problem, the symptoms listed above may appear in combination.

Behavioral Problems

The social adjustment of a German Shepherd Dog deserves proper nurturing just as any other member of the human family. Neglect, trauma or abuse, separation from its family, and even a temporary stay in a boarding kennel during your vacation, as well as inconsistent or inappropriate training can cause behavioral problems. Experiences that affect the dog in a negative way can stress the dog and trigger illness or disease. If you are experiencing behavior problems that interfere with the normal companionship and sharing of your home with your pet you will want to ask your veterinarian for a referral to an animal behaviorist. These animal behaviorists are specialists who are trained in the diagnosis and treatment including behavior modification in companion animals with behavior problems that owners are unable to handle.

Keeping Your Dog Healthy

If your pet should become ill, or if an emergency situation occurs, it is important to take a few important steps.

Visiting the Veterinarian

It is best to transport a sick dog to the veterinarian by car. Have someone ride with you to pet the dog and keep it calm.

You can help the veterinarian make a diagnosis by providing information about the dog's symptoms; therefore, you need to write down everything you have observed. Frequently, stool and urine samples will be helpful. Make a note of any medications you have given the dog, and remember to take along your pet's vaccination certificate.

Administering Medicine

Tablets can be "concealed" in a piece of spreadable meat (such as liverwurst) or placed at the very back of the dog's tongue, while you hold its mouth open. Then hold its jaws shut until it swallows. Afterward, feed the dog something moist, to keep the tablet from getting stuck in its throat.

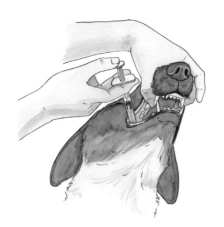

Liquid medications can be squirted into the side of the dog's mouth, between the rows of teeth, with a disposable plastic syringe (without the cannula, or tube). To do so, pull the dog's flews down slightly and raise its head.

Eyedrops can be dripped behind the lower lid. Pull the lid slightly downward.

Eye ointment can be placed, in a ribbon, inside the lower eyelid. Carefully pull the lid downward.

Taking the Dog's Temperature

Have someone familiar to the dog help you take its temperature. That person should hold it firmly around its neck and beneath its abdomen. Then you lift the dog's tail and insert the thermometer, its tip lubricated with petroleum jelly, up to one third of its length into the dog's rectum. Hold the thermometer in place while the reading is being obtained, and talk to the dog soothingly to keep it calm. Practice this procedure from time to time while performing regular grooming.

Note: Shatterproof digital thermometers that beep to signal that the readout is ready are quite handy.

Emergency Situations

Now and then emergency situations can occur in which only quick action can save the life of your dog. Be aware of the following:

Insect sting: German Shepherd Dogs are very fond of snapping at wasps or bees, and sometimes they get stung. The dog is most likely to be stung on the nose, muzzle, head, or neck.

Squirt liquid medication into one corner of the dog's mouth, raising its head slightly and directing the medication toward the back of the cheek space behind the teeth.

Home Medicine Chest

Instruments:
- one shatterproof thermometer
- one pair of curved scissors with one blunt blade and one sharp one
- one pair of scissors for cutting bandages
- one pair of tick tweezers
- one pair of tweezers with rounded tips
- two or three wooden spatulas to apply ointment
- three plastic syringes (without cannula) with a volume of 2 milliliters, 5 milliliters, and 10 milliliters, respectively, to administer medications, foods, or liquids.

Bandaging materials:
- elastic gauze bandages (2.4 and 4 inches [6 and 10 cm] wide)
- adhesive tape and Band-Aids
- surgical cotton
- gauze compresses
- one tourniquet bandage to stop bleeding.

Medications: There are no special medications or medical items—except the ones named above—necessary for a dog's medical kit. If in doubt regarding your dog's behavior, and possible illness, consult a veterinarian immediately! Handy for your first aid kit, however, are antiseptic solution, eyewash and an eyedropper, tweezers to remove splinters and such, a rectal thermometer, petroleum jelly, and possibly an emergency snakebite kit.

Note: Ask your veterinarian to recommend a place where you can get an "emergency bloat kit" and have the veterinarian instruct you in its use. The kit contains a large-diameter tube that can save the life of a dog when it has bloated and only before the torsion or twisting of the stomach has occurred. "Bloat" and "stomach torsion," also known as gastric dilatation volvulus, is a medical emergency and your dog must get to a veterinarian immediately.

There may be swelling of the nose, lips, or the area surrounding the sting, and the dog may rub or scratch at the sting site. Apply an ice bag, or ice cubes placed in a sock or wrapped in a towel, over the swollen area. Dogs may also get into nests of insects where they are stung several times by wasps, bees, or hornets on other parts of their bodies. Seek veterinary attention in these situations. Your veterinarian may want to give your dog medication such as

First aid for swelling from wasp or bee stings or traumatic injury can be applied while you seek veterinary attention.

It is easier on the joints to provide exercise on grass instead of on pavement or concrete.

Benedryl to counteract the reaction. A sting in the mouth or throat can result in swelling of the throat, difficulty breathing, weakness, disorientation, seizures, or a collapse that puts the dog's life in danger. If your dog exhibits any of these reactions, do not hesitate to get your pet to a veterinarian immediately.

Cuts on the feet: While out for a walk, a dog can very easily step on a piece of broken glass or other sharp material. A gaping wound in the pad of its foot can result, and it will bleed profusely. If that occurs, make a pressure bandage at once. You may find someone with a first aid kit in the car who can provide you with a gauze compress and a bandage. Lay the compress directly on the injured area and wrap the bandage around it. In a pinch, a paper tissue will do the job: Place it on the wound and wrap

a scrap of cloth around it. Then take the dog to the nearest veterinarian.

Bites: German Shepherd Dogs may fight. If they do have a fight, have every bite examined by your veterinarian. The opponent's tooth will have made only a small, though often very deep, hole, and after a few days a serious infection can develop. Fever, apathy, loss of appetite, and blood poisoning can be the result. Stanch heavily bleeding wounds with a pressure bandage, or use your hand to exert pressure on the blood vessel to keep the dog from bleeding to death. Get the dog to the veterinarian at once.

Poisoning: Symptoms of poisoning are heavy drooling, repeated vomiting with traces of blood, traces of blood in diarrhea and urine, pale to bluish mucous membranes, racing pulse, and/or loss of consciousness. See the veterinarian or go to an emergency clinic immediately!

Breed-Related Diseases

There are certain diseases that are not unusual in the German Shepherd Dog. Some of them are discussed in this text.

Panosteitis ("Pano")

Panosteitis (see also page 65) is a rotating lameness resulting from an inflammation of the long bones. The causes are poorly understood but it occurs more frequently in males, between the age of five months and eighteen months of age. Lameness is usually seen between five months and ten months of age, during the rapid growth of the dog, and can be precipitated by stress or strenuous activity. Lameness may shift from one leg to another. It can be quite painful, to the point of causing the dog to stop eating. In the severe manifestation it can cause muscle deterioration or atrophy. The veterinarian makes the diagnosis by X-ray or palpation. This condition should be treated aggressively to avoid gait changes and to avoid the chronic form of panosteitis. Without accurate diagnosis it can be confused with hip dysplasia.

Hip Dysplasia (HD)

HD is a malformation of the hip joint that is found not only in German Shepherd Dogs, but in many medium, large, and giant-breed dogs. While it is a genetic disease, the inheritance is complex and not yet fully understood. There are environmental influences such as excessive and intense exercise on hard surfaces (concrete, for example) in young animals and overfeeding from a young age. This causes rapid growth, and excess weight, which is hard on the joints. Conscientious breeders have reduced the incidence of HD by careful selection of breeding animals that are free from HD. The environmental influences can be minimized by keeping the dog in good lean weight and walking or playing with the young dog on grass or gravel rather than pavement or concrete until its skeleton is fully mature at the age of two.

Symptoms: As affected young animals mature, this disease is manifested in a poor fit between the acetabulum (the hip socket) and the head of the femur (the thighbone). What should be a tight-fitting ball and socket joint in the hip is not tightly fitted and results in abnormal wear and tear; premature arthritic changes develop. The gait is not smooth and elastic and the dog may "bunny-hop." The dog may be lame, may have pain, and may experience difficulty getting up and lying down and going up and down stairs. The long-range outcome of this disease is dependent upon the pain tolerance of the individual animal, and the weight and condition, medication management, and exercise routine that is provided by the owners.

Treatment: The definitive diagnosis is made by X-ray of the pelvis. Your veterinarian can prescribe medication to reduce inflammation if the dog is lame. Long-term therapy with the use of joint supplements can be started when the diagnosis is made. Most dogs can be successfully managed with a proper exercise regime. Surgical treatment can be offered in the worst cases.

Elbow Dysplasia

There is probably no single cause of elbow dysplasia and some believe that it is part of a general condition known as osteochondrosis, which is an abnormality in the growth of cartilage. There is likely to be an inheritance factor but that has not been well defined. There is thought to be a nutritional component as well. Rapid growth, excessive calories, overfeeding, and excessive weight are believed to contribute to the likelihood of developing this disease.

Symptoms: Clinical signs of elbow dysplasia usually become apparent between six and ten months of age. The lameness can be very subtle at the onset. As time goes on, arthritic changes begin to take place in the joint. Surgery may minimize the arthritic changes.

Pancreatic Insufficiency

In the typical history of a dog suffering from pancreatic exocrine insufficiency, the dog owner reports weight loss despite excessive eating. This condition may come on over a period of time. In addition to weight loss, thin appearance, and a general unthrifty look resulting from the inability to digest food, the dog will exhibit symptoms of dry skin and poor coat texture as a result of poor fat metabolism. The dog has large volumes of light-colored, unformed feces, five or more times daily. Feces have a rancid smell and a greasy texture. Dogs with this condition do not have sufficient enzymes to digest their food for absorption and nourishment. They are basically starving because they are unable to absorb the nutrients in the food. These dogs must be seen by a veterinarian. Blood work, not a fecal test, should be done to determine the amount of pancreatic enzyme typsin available in the bloodstream and if the diagnosis is confirmed, the dog will need oral enzyme supplementation.

It is known that there is a genetic predisposition to this condition in the German Shepherd Dog. It is also believed to be one of the autoimmune diseases.

Malabsorption

The symptoms are similar to those of pancreatic insufficiency and lack of pancreatic enzymes can be one factor. Other causes are intestinal worms, irritable bowel syndrome, gastric disease, or an obstructed bile duct. Irritable bowel syndrome has been treated with immunosuppressant drugs, hypoallergenic foods, and with drugs that reduce the motility of the bowel. Consult a veterinarian who is experienced in working with German Shepherd Dogs if you are confronted with these problems.

Gastric and Intestinal Disturbances

There are a number of conditions with similar symptoms that owners of German Shepherd Dogs must be aware of in order to seek emergency veterinary care when confronted with them. In seeing the first subtle signs of intestinal emergencies, the owner will need to be sensitive to these vague signs that the dog may display when something is amiss, because it is imperative to be prepared to seek emergency treatment for these most life-threatening conditions.

The conditions are as follows:

1. Gastric bloat or dilatation, a condition in which the stomach fills with air or gases.

2. Gastric volvulus or torsion, in which the stomach twists upon itself, often accompanied by bloat (gastric dilatation volvulus or GVD).

3. Splenic torsion, when the spleen twists upon itself.

4. Mesenteric torsion, in which the intestines twist on the root of the mesentery from which the intestines get their blood supply.

5. Intestinal obstruction, which is when the intestines fold in on themselves (intussusception) or when foreign matter (for example, socks or tennis balls) that the dog has ingested fails to pass through the intestines and causes a blockage.

6. Toxic gut syndrome or hemorrhagic gastroenteritis (HGE) is a disease condition precipitated by stress or a change in feeding pattern, a change in food or feeding raw or partially cooked meat, or cooked meat contaminated with the bacteria Clostridium.

Symptoms: The following symptoms are common to many of the gastric and intestinal conditions.

✔ The dog may have vomiting or regurgitation of water or foamy saliva or retching that does not bring up either food or water.

✔ The dog may appear restless, pacing about, and unable to find a comfortable position.

✔ The dog may get up and lie down repeatedly and seek contact with its human companions or may become listless or depressed.

✔ When the full-blown syndrome is manifested, the dog is in acute distress. It may sit or stand continuously in an effort to relieve pressure on the diaphragm.

✔ The tongue, gums, and the inside of the lips become very pale and if they should become cyanotic (blue), the dog may collapse within minutes. The pink color does not return to the tissue when the gums are pressed and released.

Bloat, torsion, or gastric dilatation volvulus can come on quite suddenly as a rapid enlargement of the abdomen but can also be present in a more subtle way before abdominal bloating is observed. The gastric dilatation compresses the major blood vessel. The torsion twists the vessels, the ability of the heart to pump blood is compromised, and the dog's blood pressure drops. Breathing becomes difficult because of the pressure on the diaphragm and lungs.

Bloody diarrhea may accompany the intestinal conditions but may be a late sign. It can present as an early sign of toxic gut syndrome. Many veterinarians are not familiar with the term, toxic gut syndrome, which German Shepherd Dog fanciers have become used to using for the condition otherwise known as HGE. Owners of German Shepherd Dogs should be familiar with both terms. Any dog with bloody diarrhea must be immediately seen by a veterinarian to rule out HGE.

Inflammation of the Cornea (Keratitis or Pannus)

This is a chronic superficial inflammation of the cornea that, left untreated, can result in permanent blindness from the pigmentation of the cornea. There is a superficial growth of blood vessels and an infiltration of white cells that makes it appear as if the animal has something on the surface of the eye. It is thought to be an immune-mediated disease. The treatment does not cure the disease but controls the progression of it.

Conditions of the Spine or Spinal Cord

There are conditions in the German Shepherd Dog and other breeds that originate in the spine or spinal cord and affect the way the rear legs function. These conditions have some symptoms in common and an extensive work-up, including an MRI, may be needed to make the diagnosis. Intermittent lameness in one or both rear limbs, weakness and wasting of the muscles of the rear limbs, or a stilted gait is a

Dogs who are severely affected by conditions of the spine or spinal cord get along quite well using a dog assistance cart.

common initial sign in all of these conditions as is difficulty in getting up and maintaining balance. Left untreated, there is progressive weakness in the rear limbs as well as a loss of bladder and bowel control.

Cauda Equina Syndrome

This disease of the spine results in compression of the nerves as they go through the spinal canal of the lower back. The onset of these symptoms is between three and seven years of age. It can be caused by arthritic changes, lumbosacral instability, lumbosacral stenosis, degenerative disc, infection, tumor, or ruptured disc.

Compression disease usually is painful and the dog may cry out in pain with sudden movement. It may experience a burning pain that may cause the dog to chew at his tail or rear feet.

Degenerative Myelopathy (DM)

Degenerative Myelopathy was first described as a specific degenerative neurologic disease in 1973.

It is now known that DM is an autoimmune disease in which the animal's immune system attacks its own nerve cells that make up the insulating layer around the nerve fibers. In contrast to cauda equina syndrome, DM is not painful but is a progressive weakness and is likened to the disease of multiple sclerosis in humans.

Diagnosis: While several tests including, an MRI, are needed to make the diagnosis, recent advances in diagnosis include the DM Flash test, which is offered at the University of Florida. The test demonstrates that there is a genetic marker present in those animals that have DM. The onset of DM occurs most often between the ages of four and ten, but younger dogs have been diagnosed. Other conditions such as lumbosacral stenosis or ruptured disk may occur together with DM. Diet, nutritional supplements, medication and exercise are extremely important in maintaining the well-being of DM-affected dogs. Therapeutic exercise maximizes muscle tone and maintains good circulation and condition. Research using autologous bone marrow stem cells is now being done that will determine if this is an effective treatment for DM.

Perianal Fistulas

This is thought to be an immune-mediated disease that may have a genetic component. The first sign may be that the dog licks the anal area frequently and upon inspection, the anal area is inflamed. Open sores or ulcers develop that become infected, and without treatment fistulas develop and the dog suffers considerable discomfort and pain. In recent years, the immune-suppressant drug, cyclosporin, has been used to effectively treat perianal fistulas, either alone or in combination with other drugs. Before the advent of use of this drug,

The steady gaze of a German Shepherd Dog is a window to the strength of character and courage in this breed. In its eyes, we see the soul of the dog.

surgical treatment such as cautery, excision, and even tail amputation was used unsuccessfully. Some dogs that suffer from perianal fistulas also have bowel disease or colitis, which also responds to cyclosporin therapy.

Euthanasia

There will come a time, because of discomforts of extreme age, disability, or disease, that the quality of life for your dog has diminished to the point that it is kinder to put your pet to sleep than to see it suffer. Many owners have said "I could tell it was time by the look in the eyes" when describing their recognition that the time had come to provide their beloved pet with the final gift of compassion.

As difficult as it is, it would be kindest to your pet to remain with it during the euthanasia procedure. You can pet and comfort your dog as the injection is given and the final sleep overtakes it. Children should be prepared for the passing of a pet and a card or picture given to them in the way of a memorial token helps to ease the loss. The final disposition of your German Shepherd Dog can be burial in a pet cemetery but many prefer cremation. Cremation remains can be kept or buried.

INFORMATION

International Kennel Clubs

As an address is almost invariably the home of an officer of the breed club, it is understandable that it can change as elections are held. It is wise to check with the American Kennel Club (AKC), 51 Madison Avenue, New York, NY 10038 for an update on a club's address.

German Shepherd Dog Club of America
Box 429
Applegate, CA 95703
www.gsdca.org

German Shepherd Dog Club of America—
  Working Dog Association
1699 N. Jungle Den Road #45
Astor, FL 32102
www.gsdca-wda.org

German Shepherd Dog Club of Canada
RR3#
Fergus, ON N1M 2W4
Canada
www. gsdcc.ca

American Kennel Club Headquarters
260 Madison Avenue
New York, NY 10016
Phone: (212) 696-8200
www.akc.org

American Kennel Club Operations
5580 Centerview Drive
Raleigh, NC 27606
Customer Service Phone: (919) 233-9767

AKC Companion Animal Recovery (CAR)
Phone: (800) 252-7894

American German Shepherd Rescue Association
P.O. Box 7113
Clearlake, CA 95422
Phone: (630) 529-7396
www.agsra.com

White Shepherd Clubs
www.awsaclub.com, www.wgsdca.org,
  www.whiteshepherd.org

Fédération Cynologique Internationale (FCI)
13 Place Albert I
B-6530 Thuin
Belgium

The Kennel Club
1-4 Clargis Street, Piccadilly
London W7Y 8AB
England

New Zealand Kennel Club
P.O. Box 523
Wellington, 1
New Zealand

Verein für Deutsche Schäferhunde e.v. (SV)
D-86167 Augsburg
Germany

Information and Printed Material

American Boarding Kennel Association
4575 Galley Road, Suite 400 A
Colorado Springs, Colorado 80915
www.abka.com
(Publishes lists of approved boarding kennels.)

American Veterinary Medical Association
930 North Meacham Road, Suite 100
Schaumberg, Illinois 60173
www.avma.org

Gaines TWT
P.O. Box 8172
Kankakee, Illinois 60901
(Publishes *Touring with Towser,* a directory of hotels and motels that accommodate guests with dogs.)

Books

In addition to the most recent edition of the official publication of the American Kennel Club, *The Complete Dog Book*, published by Howell Book House, New York, other suggestions include:

How to Be Your Dog's Best Friend: The Classic Training Manual for Dog Owners by the Monks of New Skete, 2002.

Alderton, David, *The Dog Care Manual.* Hauppauge, New York: Barron's Educational Series, Inc., 1986.

Antesberger, Helmut, *The German Shepherd Dog.* Hauppauge, New York: Barron's Educational Series, Inc., 1985.

Baer, Ted, *Communicating with Your Dog.* Hauppauge, New York: Barron's Educational Series, Inc., 1989.

___, *How to Teach Your Old Dog New Tricks.* Hauppauge, New York: Barron's Educational Series, Inc., 1991.

Klever, Ulrich, *The Complete Book of Dog Care.* Hauppauge, New York: Barron's Educational Series, Inc., 1989.

Rutherford, Clarice, David H. Niel. *How to Raise a Puppy You Can Live With.* Loveland, CO: Alpine Publications, 2005.

Ullmann, Hans, *The New Dog Handbook.* Hauppauge, New York: Barron's Educational Series, Inc., 1984.

Wrede, Barbara, *Civilizing Your Puppy.* Hauppauge, New York: Barron's Educational Series, Inc., 1992.

Share your life and your home with a German Shepherd Dog and you will have a trusted friend and companion for its lifetime.

INDEX

About the Authors

Horst Hegewald-Kawich has long been employed by the police as a dog handler. He also serves as a judge at dog sports tournaments and as an examiner of dogs for the blind. Ginny Altman was president of The German Shepherd Dog Club of America, Inc. in 2004–2005 and was on the Board of Directors from 1998–2003. In 1992, she was licensed by the American Kennel Club to judge German Shepherd Dogs; today, she is licensed to judge 12 of the herding breeds.

Cover Photos

Karen Hudson: front cover; Isabelle Francais: back cover, inside front cover, inside back cover.

Important Note

This pet owner's guide tells the reader how to buy and care for a German Shepherd Dog. The authors and the publisher consider it important to point out that the guidelines presented in this book apply primarily to normally developed dogs from a reputable breeder—that is, to dogs in good health and of good character.

Anyone who adopts an adult dog should be aware that its personality might already have been influenced by other people. If possible, meet the previous owner and assess the interaction between the owner and the dog. If there is an affectionate relationship between them, you can be assured that, given some adjustment time, the dog will bond to you in the same way. If the dog comes from an animal shelter or rescue organization, the personnel in those organizations are trained to assess the personalities of dogs that come to them. Dogs with severe behavioral problems that cannot adapt to a new environment are not offered for adoption by either animal shelters or rescue organizations. Rescue organizations place dogs in homes with experienced owners, where they are evaluated, trained as necessary, and kept until they are placed as pets in permanent homes.

Animal shelters and rescue organizations see to it that the dog has all the necessary immunizations. If you are acquiring an adult dog from a private party be sure to get all of the health records from the previous owner. In any case, you will want to make arrangements to have your pet seen by your veterinarian before long.

Even well-behaved and carefully supervised dogs sometimes do damage to someone else's property or cause accidents. It is therefore in the owner's interest to be adequately insured against such eventualities, and we strongly urge all dog owners to purchase a liability policy that covers their dog(s).

Photo Credits

Ginny Altman: 15, 16 (bottom), 71, and 77; Tara Darling: 4, 5, 6 (bottom), 8 (bottom), 12 (top and bottom), 13, 17 (top and bottom), 19, 21 (bottom), 22, 26 (top), 29, 30, 31, 35, 37, 38, 40, 41, 43, 54, 55, 56, 57, 67, 69, 78, 90, and 93; Isabelle Francais: 6 (top), 9 (left and right), 10, 11, 16 (top), 18, 20, 21 (top), 23, 25, 26 (bottom), 27, 28, 32 (top and bottom), 34, 39, 44, 46, 51, 60, 61, 63, 64, 65, 68, 73, 76, 82, 83, and 86; and Karen Hudson: 2–3, 7, 8 (top), 14, 33, 62, 81, and 91.

German edition © Copyright 1995 by Gräfe und Unzer Verlag GmbH, Munich, Germany.
Original German title: *Der deutsche Schaferhund.*

All inquiries should be addressed to:
Barron's Educational Series, Inc.
250 Wireless Boulevard
Hauppauge, NY 11788
www.barronseduc.com

ISBN-13: 978-0-7641-3457-9
ISBN-10: 0-7641-3457-4

Library of Congress Catalog Card No. 2006042954

Library of Congress Cataloging-in-Publication Data
Hegewald-Kawich, Horst.
[Deutsche Schaferhund. English]
The German shepherd dog : everything about purchase, care, feeding, and training / Horst Hegewald-Kawich and Ginny Altman ; illustrations by Michele Earle-Bridges.
    p. cm.
ISBN-13: 978-0-7641-3457-9 (alk. paper)
ISBN-10: 0-7641-3457-4 (alk. paper)
1. German shepherd dog. I. Altman, Ginny. II. Title.

SF429.G37H4413   2006
636.737'6—dc22   2006042954

Printed in China
9 8